"My God, he's done it! D. B. Gilles has topped himself I previously felt nothing can be better than his first book c now comes out with the second edition of Better wisdom, laughs, and heart! Read the contents pages of D. B. Gilles' te Within, 2nd Edition. You'll be hooked forever

D0091318

> — Dr. Lew Hunter, screenwriter, author of Lew Hunter's Screenwriting 434, Chairman, UCLA Screenwriting Department

"The 2nd edition of Screenwriter Within is just as knowledgeable and fun as D. B.'s screenwriting classes, with real-world insights into the life of a professional writer and working in Hollywood."

> — David Benullo, writer, Around the World in 80 Days, The Dead Zone

"As trustworthy a guide as ever, D. B. not only delivers solid commentary about the creative writing process, he also addresses the shifting realities of how deals get made. Solid insights for anyone plotting a path into the movie and television trade."

> — David McKenna, co-author, Memo from the Story Department

"The new updated edition of The Screenwriter Within should come with 3-D glasses and popcorn it's so good. Packed with the latest essential information for the current screenwriting market, it's smart, cool, and cutting-edge."

> — Sheldon Woodbury, screenwriting professor, New York University; author, Cool Million, How to Become A Million Dollar Screenwriter

"Trust me: D. B.'s book will help you navigate and finish a professionally developed and structured screenplay, no matter what your previous experience."

> — Dan Pulick, co-writer, Fanboys

"The Screenwriter Within, 2nd Edition, is a writer's dream — a screenwriting book that makes you excited to sit down and write."

> — Andrew Chambliss, writer, The Vampire Diaries; Spartacus: Blood & Sand; Dollhouse

"Where most screenwriting books teach you form or style, D. B. takes it a step further and teaches you how to be a professional screenwriter. For first-timers and seasoned pros, The Screenwriter Within is a valuable asset."

> — John Hlavin, writer, Underworld 4: New Dawn (Lakeshore/Screen Gems), The Shield (FX)

"Most books on screenwriting teach you something, but the second edition of *The Screenwriter Within* teaches you everything a screenwriter in the 21st century needs to know!"

— Mick Casale, head of Screenwriting, Graduate Film,
Tisch School of The Arts, NYU

"*The Screenwriter Within, 2nd Edition,* is an invaluable tool, and D. B. always keeps you engaged with his incredible sense of humor."

— Andrew Gurland, writer, *The Last Exorcism,*
writer/director, *The Virginity Hit*

"You won't find a better book that focuses on the basics (and more) than *The Screenwriter Within, 2nd Edition.* Written with humor, honesty and clarity — it will truly help you improve your screenplay."

— Matthew Terry, filmmaker; screenwriter; teacher;
columnist for www.hollywoodlitsales.com

"Of all the screenwriting professors I know, D. B. Gilles' methodology is the most fun to read and the most practical. About movies and the movie business, William Goldman once famously said, 'No one knows anything.' *The Screenwriter Within, 2nd Edition,* proves Goldman wrong. Gilles knows about screenwriting and his book is as helpful as it gets."

— Amos Poe, filmmaker, screenwriter

"Hollywood demystified! In *The Screenwriter Within, 2nd Edition,* D. B. Gilles provides you with the keys to the kingdom, then tells you how to use them."

— Gail Gilchriest, writer, *My Dog Skip, The Ponder Heart,*
*The Greening of Whitney Brown*

"Take this one to your favorite coffee shop and prepare to hang out for a couple of hours with the wisest, funniest, most grounded-in-reality screenwriting coach you can imagine. In these short, incisive chapters you'll get a lifetime's worth of insider tips and common-sense strategies for mastering the screenwriting game."

— Christopher Vogler, author, *The Writer's Journey;*
co-author, *Memo from the Story Department*

"Gilles is an absolute master when it comes to showing you how to develop story. He walks you through it in a simple, concise, and clear approach that will spawn many "aha" moments. I believe this new edition of *The Screenwriter Within* is one of the best screenwriting books out there. It will inspire screenwriters at every level to know what it will take to turn their story into a sale."

— Jen Grisanti, author, *Story Line: Finding Gold in Your*
*Life Story;* writing instructor for Writers on the Verge with NBC

# THE SCREEN-WRITER WITHIN

2ND EDITION

D.B. GILLES

### NEW STRATEGIES TO FINISH YOUR SCREENPLAY & GET A DEAL!

Published by Michael Wiese Productions
12400 Ventura Blvd. #1111
Studio City, CA 91604
tel. 818.379.8799
fax 818.986.3408
mw@mwp.com
www.mwp.com

Cover design: Johnny Ink *www.johnnyink.com*
Book design: Gina Mansfield Design
Editor: PJ Dempsey

Printed by McNaughton & Gunn, Inc., Saline, Michigan
Manufactured in the United States of America

© 2011 by D. B. Gilles

Library of Congress Cataloging-in-Publication Data

Gilles, D. B.
  The screenwriter within : new strategies to finish your screen-play & get a deal / D. B. Gilles. -- 2nd ed.
      p. cm.
  ISBN 978-1-61593-057-9
  1. Motion picture authorship. 2. Television authorship. I. Title.
PN1996.G44 2011
808.2'3--dc22
                                                        2011017405

*for*
Jane Terese Campbell

■ ■ ■

# Contents

# Special Acknowledgements

Josephine Gilles, my mother, for encouraging me to take typing lessons in high school; Janet Neipris, mentor and friend; Jane Dystel, my literary agent, for her belief in the idea; PJ Dempsey, my editor, for her guidance and input; Venable Herndon; Sheldon Woodbury for consistently intelligent criticism; Don DeMaio for friendship and philosophical conversations; my sister, Kathy, for always being there for me; Margo Haas for friendship and belief since the early days. To my students, friends, and colleagues at Tisch School of the Arts, New York University.

# Foreword

## What the New *Screenwriter Within* Means to You

Since the first edition of *The Screenwriter Within* was published in 2000, I've received thousands of emails, phone calls, and texts from screenwriters who read the book, my articles, or my blog, *Screenwriters Rehab*.

I listened to their concerns, questions, and feedback, gave it serious thought, and incorporated the input into this new edition with approximately 70% new and revised material.

If you're new to screenwriting and about to start your first screenplay, if you've written several scripts, if you're a fan of the first edition, if you never heard of it, or if you're seeking a new career path and thinking of being a screenwriter, you'll find this updated version of *The Screenwriter Within* to be a valuable guide.

Just as the world has changed since the book was first published, so has the plight of the screenwriter, both new and not-so-new.

Why? Because the movie-making business has also changed.

I've changed too. I've gotten wiser and savvier about how the business of screenwriting works, both as a writer myself, as well as a teacher and writing coach.

The key to success in any profession is learning how to adapt. That certainly applies to screenwriting.

In the past, there was a clear differentiation between the studio film (mainstream Hollywood) and the independent film world. Now it's pretty much overlapping. Major stars, directors, and established screenwriters are making "smaller" films. Not only that, but many screenwriters are turning to television, particularly those who write dramas, because TV has become more receptive to drama while Hollywood has not. Notwithstanding the fact that dramas tend to win Oscars: Don't get me started.

Scripts that would've been made twenty (or even ten) years ago might not have a chance now. Much like the world we live in, comedies are less innocent. Teenagers and pre-teens are more worldly and sophisticated (but not necessarily smarter) because of the constant flow of media and pop culture information. Stuff they would've liked in the past bores them now. They need edgier stuff.

Studios are looking for "product" that can reach all ages. That's why there are so many animated films. In the past they were few and far between. Not anymore. Studios have found pay dirt in the genre. Little kids love 'em, as do big kids, adults, parents, and grandparents. If you can get *everybody* into the theater, life is good. Make only animated films!

Fortunately, movies made specifically for television are still a viable option. There are Lifetime, ABC Family, MTV, and the occasional HBO or Showtime original movies, but the market is dwindling.

Consider the new technology. On one end you've got *Avatar*. On the other end you've got high def digital cameras that are so inexpensive to use that it's virtually impossible to tell if a film was shot on the cheap.

In the past, if a film went straight to video it was an embarrassment to everyone concerned, especially the writer. But that's all changed. We've become a Netflix society. It's so easy to watch movies online now. Who needs to go to a video store anymore?

And who knows if Netflix will be around in five years? It might be superseded by something more technologically advanced. And of course, there's On Demand. And lots of people buy DVDs. One way or another, a studio will make a profit.

Star-driven vehicles are failing. Look back to the pivotal summer of 2010. *Knight and Day* with Tom Cruise and *Killers* with Katherine Heigl and Ashton Kutcher both tanked at the box office. Until *Inception*, Leonardo DiCaprio had a few consecutive box office duds.

Does this mean the star system is failing? That could be a good thing. No longer will a studio pay an actor/actress a small fortune if there's a chance the movie will bomb. Instead of looking for star vehicles, maybe studios will just look for good material, i.e., your screenplay will be the star.

More than ever, studios are looking for franchises, and in doing so they are turning to comic book heroes, old TV shows, and graphic novels for material, rather than placing a big emphasis on original material. That's bad. They're looking for a pre-sold audience.

In the past, a screenwriter could send a query letter containing a brief logline of a script to an agent and get it read. That's pretty much over. Secretaries and assistants are instructed to toss them or return them unopened. There was a time during the last ten years where you might be able to reach an agent or manager through email. Those days are gone too, for the most part, primarily because it's become impossible to find the email address of someone who can help you. Getting one of those available-to-the-public *info@ nameofagency.com* addresses won't do you any good. And if you should get hold of a valid address for an agent, your message will be blocked unless your own address is already in her address book.

A screenwriter wanting to get a foothold in the business these days has to be smarter now. You need to know how to find that unfindable email address and it isn't easy. You need to figure out which up-and-coming agents will read your script or at least read your logline.

All is not lost though. Websites like *Inktip.com*, *Scriptpimp.com*, *Scriptshark.com*, and others provide a place for screenwriters to showcase their work.

These days, a screenplay has to be as close to the goal line as possible when you send it out to an agent, manager, or producer. You can't just submit a solid draft that your friends and family like, or that the people in your screenwriting workshop or support group loved.

It has to be so good that you'll knock the socks off whoever's reading it.

To help you achieve that and to aid you in learning how to be more informed about the business, the new version of *The Screenwriter Within* delivers the latest, most useful information.

# Introduction

I've read more than 3,000 screenplays, treatments, and out-
lines — not to mention hundreds of spec scripts — for
television, as well as novels and plays.

Besides being on the faculty of the Maurice Kanbar
Institute of Film & Television at New York University's
Tisch School of the Arts, I've been a script consultant and
writing coach for many years. I advise screenwriters on
how to write and complete a script or improve their already
completed screenplays.

I guarantee clients two things: If they listen to me I'll
show them how to make their scripts better and bring them
closer to the goal line. I never promise that they'll make a
sale because that's in the hands of the gods. I've worked with
fledgling (and experienced) screenwriters of all ages from all
over the world.

I've learned that we all have a story to tell. I know that
the lessons, insights, and strategies I share in this book will
help you tell yours and get acquainted with the screenwriter
within you.

Based on my years as a teacher and script consultant,
as well as a writer, I've learned that many people writing
screenplays have never properly learned how to be a screenwriter. In fact, *being* a screenwriter is much more difficult
than writing a screenplay. I know from personal experience.
I've written eight, had three optioned, sold two and had one
made. If someone is doing it right, being a screenwriter is
an all-consuming job in and of itself. Just as a screenwriter

learns how to write a screenplay by doing it, the same must be said of learning how to *be* a screenwriter; by doing it. But if you don't know how, you'll be at a disadvantage in the Hollywood of today.

You need more than a good or great script. You need a strategy and a game plan.

Sophocles had a nice take on the subject of learning by doing:

*One must learn by doing the thing;*
*for though you think you know it,*
*you have no certainty until you try.*

*The Screenwriter Within* will give you what you need to know about writing, rewriting, polishing, and completing your screenplay, as well as providing a crash course in helping you learn how to walk the walk, talk the talk, and avoid the traps screenwriters face in Hollywood today.

*D. B. Gilles*

New York City

# How the Book Works

Chapters are of varying length. They are as long or short as it takes to get the information across. Some make their point within two pages. Others take more. Some call for writing exercises, others do not.

Some of the thoughts I wanted to convey didn't merit their own chapters, but needed to be mentioned and learned. To accommodate them, I've included numerous small but crucial tips called "Strategies."

They appear between each chapter. Most stand alone in their content. A few provide additional spin on a point previously mentioned. Think of them as an easy-reference troubleshooting guide to turn to while you're writing first drafts and especially during rewrites and polishes.

In Part 5 you'll find expanded strategies called "Game Plans" that will teach you to be more professional and Hollywood-savvy.

*"Whatever you can do, or dream
you can, begin it."*
— John Wolfgang von Goethe

■ ■ ■

*"How long does it take to learn
poker, Dad?" "All your life, son."*
— David Spanier, *Total Poker*

# PART 1
# STORY
# TELLING

*"Some movies are released, others escape."*

— Hollywood Wisdom

■ ■ ■

*"One's real life is so often the life that one does not lead."*

— Oscar Wilde

CHAPTER 1

# Start Smart: The Punctuation Theory of Screenwriting

*"For the things we have to learn before we can do them, we learn by doing them."*

— Aristotle

Completing the first draft of your screenplay is your primary goal. Without it you can't begin to rethink, revise, rewrite, and polish it into a script that has a chance of being sold or optioned, or of getting you representation or a producer who might take an interest in you.

The first step to getting to the *end* of your first draft is to learn how to begin it.

The most important idea you should retain from this book is the Punctuation Theory of Screenwriting.

## Act I Ends With a ?

A man (the hero) meets a woman who is married. (Instigating Event) But her marriage is an unhappy one, so they begin a torrid love affair. Will they get caught and, if so, will there be consequences? (Major Dramatic Question introduced.)

Think of the Instigating Event as the thing that happens that causes the rest of the story to happen.

Think of the Major Dramatic Question as the one thing the audience wants to know.

## Act II Ends With an !

The man finds out the woman isn't married to an ordinary guy. Her husband is a hit man for the mob who is incredibly jealous and ruthless. (New Information) Will our hero run for his life or fight for her?

The New Information is the !

It is also the Turning Point for your hero. Because he loves the woman he will most certainly fight for her and this leads us into Act III. Only now, the stakes have been raised.

## Act III Ends With a ▪

The hero must find a way to save not only the woman he loves, but himself, as well as guaranteeing a safe future for them. In doing so he reveals his identity to the hit man, who is now out for blood.

He wants both the hero and the woman dead. The hero finds a way to save them both and eliminate the hit man. He does so and the two live happily ever after. Or he dies so that she may live. Or she dies so that he may live. But one way or another, the story has ended.

The Major Dramatic Question has been answered. Resolution. The story is over.

Unfortunately, this simple thesis is surprisingly difficult to pull off, but once you understand its underlying wisdom, even before you start writing your screenplay, you'll be at an advantage. More about this in subsequent chapters.

### Doing the Math

I failed Algebra my freshman year of high school and Geometry my sophomore year. Other than the embarrassment of flunking and the fact that I had to retake both classes during summer school, I remember not being all that worried. I assumed I would never have any use for either discipline in my life.

I was right. To this day I have never utilized anything I learned (or didn't learn) in those two classes.

I can add, subtract, multiply, and divide. I seldom find myself in situations where I have to "divide" anything and multiplying isn't something I do that often.

Subtraction and addition come in handy when I balance my checkbook or tally up a check in a restaurant.

It wasn't until I began teaching that the value of mathematics hit me.

There's an understanding in Hollywood that a screenplay has three acts and that most scripts come in at anywhere from 100 to 120 pages. Screenplays are broken down into three acts, although I've seen some segmented into five acts and others (typically movies for television) into seven acts. I prefer the three-act breakdown.

What is an "act?" By definition, an act is one of the principal divisions of a theatrical work, originating with plays and operas. As movies came along after plays and operas it was only natural that screenplays were also separated into acts.

In my teaching and script consulting experience, I've noticed that most people have a problem figuring out where the act breaks should fall. This is a problem for almost everyone, even people with a firm understanding of structure.

After reading dozens of screenplays that became films, I began to see a pattern. Act I tended to end anywhere from page 30 to 35. Act II tended to end somewhere between page 82 and 90, and Act III ran from about page 91 to 120. It was the traditional 120-page screenplay format. (Note: In the actual filmed versions of most screenplays, time-wise, the end of Act I usually comes within the first thirty-seven to forty-two minutes of the movie.)

I do it a little differently. I encourage people to shoot for 110 pages in their first drafts. Why this number? Screenplays should not be more than 120 pages. By aiming for 110 pages you have wiggle room. Using 120 pages as a destination gives you no room to breathe if your screenplay is coming in too long. By aiming for 110 pages, if you absolutely need more pages you can add them. But aim for 120 pages, and if you need more pages you'll go over the limit and then have to find 10-pages worth of what you have written and cut them.

The 110-page destination also works well if your screenplay isn't long enough. If you're about to write FADE OUT on page 87, it's too short. Psychologically, by aiming for 110 pages, you can push yourself to crack the 100- to 103-page barrier.

Figure that if your final draft is between 100 and 110 pages, you're in good shape. And if your final draft needs to be longer, anywhere between 110 and 120 pages will work.

By utilizing the Punctuation Theory, it becomes easy to pinpoint where the act breaks should occur.

And by forcing yourself to remember that the **?** should be presented between pages 30 and 32 (ideally page 30) and that the **!** should fall around page 82, you won't find yourself having a first act that ends too early (say, page 23) or comes too late (say, page 48). And you won't have a third act that comes in too early at page 74 or too late at page 103.

## A Few MoreThoughts on Math

Every screenplay in progress is filled with walls that every screenwriter either smashes into head-on or is blindsided by. Some are made of iron, some of granite, but most are sand.

Wet sand. Lots of wet sand.

The first wall usually comes around page 20. This is the place where many a new (or even experienced) screenwriter is ready to throw in the towel.

"I hate my idea," is the most common excuse given.

"I have a new idea that's better," is another justification I hear over and over.

My response is always the same. "If you quit now you'll hate your new idea on page 20 of that script and you'll want to start another idea which you'll hate when you come to page 20 on it, and you'll spend weeks (or months) making false starts and winding up with 60 to 80 pages of abandoned scripts."

Unless a screenwriter has tackled a monumentally complicated idea that requires more experience, I never encourage starting something fresh. Breaking through, climbing over, sneaking around, or digging under the page 20 wall is a rite of passage.

Periodically, one hears the story about a screenwriter who churns out a high six-figure script in eight days or three weeks or some maddeningly speedy time frame. But the fact is, 99% of screenplays aren't written fast and I know enough screenwriters to back this up.

You should expect about three walls in your script. For me, page 20 is the most common, then around page 50, and then around the end of Act II on page 82. And understand that there is great satisfaction in getting through them.

Giving up and starting a new script won't do much for your confidence. And as a screenwriter you'll need all the self-esteem and confidence you can get.

# Strategy

## Every Screenplay You Start
## Is Like a New Relationship

Screenwriting is like dating. You meet someone (you get an idea). Being with your new lover is so easy (the first 15 pages almost write themselves). Things look incredibly promising for the first four weeks (Act I is done and Act II is so well-thought-out you could write it in your sleep.) Then a reality check hits you in the face. You find out your new soul mate has a nasty little cocaine addiction/gave you an STD/is married/is a pre-op transsexual/doesn't really like children, dogs, cats, your friends, your hobbies. (The structure that seemed so right suddenly falls apart/your main character is boring/the dialogue is stilted/unfunny/dumb and you have no third act and no ending and the most appealing character was killed off in the middle of Act II.) When your relationship/screenplay hits a wall you have two choices: end it, find someone new, and try again (abandon it, find a new idea, and start all over) or try to break down the wall by working through the problems. Unless you're in love with the person, end it. (Unless you're in love with the idea, abandon it.) Because even when you're in love with someone (or a script), it's hard enough to make it work.

## Writing Exercise

Write a two-page essay about the worst thing that ever happened to your family. A divorce, a death, violence, alcoholism, i.e., something bad. Then dramatize it into a 5- to 7-page screenplay in which one character talks about the effect of the bad thing on his/her life.

CHAPTER 2

# You Can't Have a Plot Without Things Happening

*"With a tale, forsooth, he cometh unto you, with a
tale that holdeth children play and old men from the
chimney corner."*

— Sir Philip Sidney

Drama is revelation.

Your story must move forward. Things must happen.
You can't just have your characters talking about nothing.
What they say and do must further the dramatic tension of
the story. This is what plotting is. Just as we plan the events
of a special evening, we must "plan" our screenplays.

Many times you'll find yourself with a situation, but
not a story. For example, a nun wants to leave the convent a
few days before she's to take her final vows. Okay. By itself,
that's not particularly dramatic. It's a situation. It becomes
a story when we learn that the reason she wants to leave is
because she's been hiding out in the convent. Why? Because
she committed a crime two years before and now she feels
the coast is clear. Or because she's fallen in love with a priest.
Or another nun. With any of these scenarios it becomes a
story.

Whether you're writing an action/adventure that requires
the proverbial thrill-a-minute or a gentle tale about two

souls wounded by life who find each other, you must keep the story moving. There must be dramatic tension.

You must have pivotal plot points. They are the key events that move the story forward and provide important information. Think in terms of cause and effect. This happens, then that happens, then this happens. Every few pages make sure something is happening.

When I read a screenplay I make notes on the pages where something pivotal happens. I'll write out the words Key Plot Point or Key Information. If too many pages pass without something pivotal happening, your story has stopped moving forward.

If you've written a batch of pages (say five to ten) and nothing is happening (meaning the story isn't moving forward and we aren't learning anything important about the protagonist), this is problematic, even if your dialogue is brilliant and your stage directions sheer poetry.

Your protagonist must be talking about and/or doing things that are organic to the story or character development. If all you've accomplished is to show us the minutiae of your protagonist's morning ritual from the ring of the alarm clock, to how long she shampoos her hair, to how thoroughly she flosses her teeth after breakfast, you've shown us (pardon my Zen) both too much and not enough. You will lose us.

If you want to spend time showing your main character preparing her breakfast, do so only if what she eats will make a statement about who she is. Whole-wheat toast without butter and instant coffee with milk doesn't say much. But if you have her carefully trim the crust off the toast, then slice it into triangular-shaped pieces, then arrange them on a plate in the shape of a pentagram, then have her recite a witchlike chant in which she praises the God of Wheat Fields, then you've dramatized something important about her character.

Her breakfast ritual becomes a pivotal plot point. And if your story has her meeting the man of her dreams on her way to work, the way she meets him becomes a pivotal plot point. And as a result of meeting him, her daily routine is changed. She can't get him out of her mind. She tells a co-worker about the guy and the co-worker encourages her to try to meet him again the next morning. This is another pivotal plot point.

The next morning when we see her wake up, maybe she takes more time choosing an outfit, fixing her makeup, combing her hair, all with the intention of bumping into the guy again, only this time the guy doesn't show. Another pivotal plot point. She's bummed out. But she still can't get the guy out of her head. So from this point on all of her dramatic actions revolve around her desire to see him again. It's what she talks about. Now, she can talk about other things (her job, sick father, the brother she doesn't get along with, her interests — whatever) and through this dialogue we will learn more about her, but her primary behavior must be about meeting this guy again.

Once she meets him, you're on to the next set of pivotal plot points revolving around whether or not he'll be interested in her, and if they'll have a relationship. Once this happens, then it's just more... *this* happens, then *that* happens, then — you get the idea.

# Strategy

## Drama Requires a Character to Experience a Change of Fortune

Aristotle called it *peripeteia* and the English spelling is *peripety*. They mean "a sudden and unexpected change of fortune or reverse of circumstances."

It's always compelling to watch a character undergo a change or experience that affects the way she goes about living her life. The beautiful, mean woman gets in a car accident and is horribly scarred. How will she deal with being unattractive and no longer popular? How will the pro-life activist react when she's raped and finds herself pregnant with the child of a psychotic, violent man with a genetic disorder? How does the high school pitching star with a 100 mile-an-hour fastball and a multi-million dollar offer from the New York Yankees handle life when he shatters his throwing arm on the eve of his signing?

Think certainty to uncertainty. Confidence to self-doubt. Love to hate.

## Writing Exercise

No matter what the genre, there must be an equally compelling protagonist. Make a list of your ten favorite movies; then, if they're not fresh in your mind, watch them again and write down what the story is and what your main character wants.

Look at how the protagonist and his primary *want* is introduced. Write down the obstacles before him. The best screenplays do a fine job of setting everything up early on so a reader or audience can sit back and wait to see how the main character will go about getting what he wants.

Then look at your screenplay(s) and see how well you've done.

CHAPTER 3

# How High
# Is Your Concept?

*"The play's the thing."*
— William Shakespeare

The term "high concept" has permeated mainstream Hollywood since roughly the early 1980s. Simply, it's the catchy one-sentence description of a screenplay's plot that encapsulates the story so succinctly that anyone can envision the whole movie.

But what is it?

The best explanation I ever heard of high concept was that when you hear it you smile and say, "Aaahhhhh, yes!" In the last decade, being able to communicate a premise in more than one sentence has become acceptable (maybe a few sentences), but there's nothing like hearing an idea in one sentence that gets across a commercial story.

Here are a few of my favorites:

*Liar, Liar*

A lawyer who is a pathological liar can't lie for 24 hours because of a birthday wish made by his son that comes true, forcing him to tell the truth in all situations.

*Galaxy Quest*

The aging cast of a once popular cult space TV show reduced to attending sci-fi conventions have to play their roles as the real thing when an alien race needs their help.

*Snakes on a Plane*

Hundreds of snakes are released on a plane in order to kill a witness being transported under police guard to testify at a trial.

*Tootsie*

An actor unable to find employment dons a dress, wig, and makeup, presents himself as an actress and becomes a huge soap opera star.

Now let's jump back a few years. Actually, a few hundred years. Actually, a few thousand years.

*Oedipus Rex* (Sophocles, 429 B.C.)

A man murders his father and marries his mother.

*Lysistrata* (Aristophanes, 411 B.C.)

An anti-war farce in which women deny their husbands sex until they stop fighting a war.

*The Orestes Trilogy: Agamemnon, The Libation Bearers,* and *The Eumenides* (Aeschylus, 458 B.C.)

A king, Agamemnon, returns home and is murdered by his faithless wife. His son, Orestes, avenges Agamemnon's murder by slaying his mother and her lover. Orestes is punished by the avenging goddesses, the Erinyes, who pursue him until he is cleansed of his blood guilt and set free.

*Romeo and Juliet* (Shakespeare, 1597)

Two teenagers from families who don't get along fall in love and, rather than be apart, take their own lives.

*Love's Labour's Lost* (Shakespeare, 1598)

Three scholars give up the pursuit of romance in the quest for knowledge.

*Hamlet* (Shakespeare, 1599–1601)

A distraught prince talks to his father's ghost and solves his father's murder.

Shakespeare, Sophocles, Aristophanes, and other playwrights in ancient Greece and Elizabethan England wrote high concept material. Much of it (which has stood the test of time and is studied in classrooms worldwide) is about topics that still fascinate today's audiences:

• adultery • ghosts • incest • insanity
• matricide • patricide • racism • rape

In short, all the dark, horrifying things some men and women do that make life so treacherous.

Let's call a spade a spade: What works in Hollywood today worked in Athens, Rome, and Stratford-upon-Avon way back when.

If there's a lesson to be learned from this, it's simply that the best stories seem to be about big issues, and the big issues, in one form or another, tend to deal with love, death, greed, power, envy, betrayal, and hatred.

However, for big issues to be dramatized, they need to be wrapped around a story that, by its very nature, makes an agent want to represent it, a producer want to buy it, and a studio want to make it. And, of course, makes an audience want to see it.

# Strategy

## Be *Sure* Your Protagonist Is Interesting

He doesn't have to be likable. She doesn't have to be a nice person. But they have to be someone a reader/audience wants to spend time with, whether it's the ninety minutes or so it takes to read a screenplay or the two hours it takes to watch the film. I can't emphasize enough the value of giving characters, main or secondary, shadings and contours. Don't make them too nice or holier than thou. Quirks help. They humanize a character.

What you despise or laugh at in other people you can give to your characters to make them richer, more complicated, and entertaining. Human beings are complex. Some more so than others, but human beings also have bad habits, eccentric rituals, and obsessive/compulsive behaviors. There's nothing like revealing a character's weak spots, foibles, eccentricities, and good old weird behavior to tantalize an audience.

Make a list of five things you do that are perfectly normal to you, but make other people think you're nuts. Here's my list:

1) Letting my dog kiss me on the mouth.

2) Having a morbid fascination with old cemeteries and celebrity graves.

3) Eating cereal at night in lieu of a fattening dessert.

4) Buying new clothes and not wearing them for a year.

5) Going to movies only in the daytime (and I mean never, *never* at night) when there aren't many people in the theater, because I hate crowds and people talking.

This stuff isn't all that weird, but it's not exactly typical. A friend of mine's idea of a snack is to eat cookie dough raw. Another friend's favorite part of a chicken dinner isn't the white or dark meat or a breast or thigh, but the skin. My sister won't eat kidney beans, so when she has chili she picks them out of her bowl.

Readers and audiences remember quirks and quirky behavior because they humanize a character.

## Writing Exercise

Practice writing compelling action/stage directions. Anyone can write a bunch of words in great detail. The skilled screenwriter does it cinematically. Describe the bedrooms of three teenagers:

1) a studious, introverted 15-year-old girl

2) a 17-year-old jock

3) a 16-year-old slacker/stoner boy

CHAPTER 4

# What We Know Isn't Very Interesting, So We Have to Make Stuff Up

*"No mask like open truth to cover lies, as to go naked is the best disguise."*

— William Congreve

The first of my three wives was the daughter of a fortune-teller in a third-rate traveling carnival that set up its tents in my hometown in Alaska during the summer after my high school graduation.

She was born in Trinidad and liked to boast that she was part Italian, part African, part American Indian, and the rest Haitian. Despite the fact that she only had one eye, blue like Paul Newman's (she covered her bad eye with a black silk patch), she was gorgeous. She also enjoyed bragging about the fact that her father was a practitioner of voodoo and black magic.

Her name was Jullanja, she was nine years older than I and had been married two times before. Both of her husbands had died mysteriously after she had taken out life insurance policies on them. I didn't know that until three days after our wedding when she asked me to sign a life insurance policy in the amount of $75,000.

I signed it for the same reason I married her. Because she asked me to. I had never had a girlfriend before and here was this older woman, very attractive and sexy in a *Hee Haw* kind of trailer trash way.

Anyway, I left my family for my new wife with the idea that I would become an integral part of the traveling carnival. Jullanja told me that the new guys always worked with the snakes, some of which were poisonous. She told me that her previous husbands worked with the snakes and that they made it through just fine.

So I started my apprenticeship with the carnival feeding, washing, and generally looking after sixteen reptiles.

I became friendly with Omar, the snake charmer, and it was he who warned me that my wife was going to do to me what she did to her first two husbands, namely, kill me.

I didn't believe him. I was in love. And I was getting sex on a regular basis. And ...

I made all of this up.

What really happened during the summer after I graduated from high school was so boring that I forgot it as I was living it. The only thing I remember happening was getting a bad sunburn.

In an era of comic book movies, screenwriters have to put their imaginations in high gear.

Most screenwriters are couch potatoes. We'd rather watch movies or read screenplays or discuss movies and would be quite happy if we never had to leave our homes.

The days of the adventurer/writer like Jack London and Ernest Hemingway don't really apply to screenwriters today. Most of the screenwriters I know either have degrees up the wazoo and never worked at anything more strenuous than being a stock boy at The Gap or maybe flipping burgers at McDonald's.

What we know and lived is pretty ordinary and uneventful, so we have to plug in our imaginations and make stuff up.

But while you're busy trying to come up with the fictions that will make up your story and main characters, don't forget to continue to draw from your personal experiences, as well as all that you have observed.

What we know and what we observe should be the foundation of character. It's your capacity to be creative that will give you the strongest ideas for your screenplay.

# Strategy

### There's the Screenplay You Sell and the Screenplay That Gets Made

Before any producer or studio shells out cash for a script, somebody has to read it. Then somebody else and somebody else. If you're lucky, only a few people will read it before a decision to represent or buy it is reached. The point is, write a script that's fun to read. Make it a page-turner. Don't go crazy with longwinded, overwhelming action/stage directions. Don't make the people reading your script work too hard. Make sure your script hooks the reader from the first page. Set a tone quickly that says, "This is going to be a fun ride." Then make it one for the rest of the screenplay.

# Writing Exercise

Practice writing in a concise, disciplined, less-is-more style. Lean dialogue, spare action/stage directions. Write three short scripts of different lengths that would be right for *Funny or Die*:

1) 1 minute with only one character

2) 5 minutes with only two characters

3) 10 minutes with more than two characters

CHAPTER 5

# Dig Deep into Your Baggage and You Might Find Gold

*"To regret one's own experiences is to arrest one's own development. To deny one's own experiences is to put a lie into the lips of one's life. It is no less than a denial of the soul."*

— Oscar Wilde

Imagine that I'm sitting across from you and piled up behind me are several large suitcases and a couple of steamer trunks.

It's my history.

My baggage.

You have baggage too, but some of us have more because we're older and have been through more. That also means some people's baggage is probably more interesting — again, because they've been through more.

You know what baggage is: the good, the bad, the ugly, the neurotic, and all the weird little idiosyncrasies we come to know about ourselves and deny. With the passing of time we also accept and understand them. Hopefully we've learned something from them. This allows us to create more fully developed, three-dimensional, nuanced characters.

The curse of youth is a tendency to see things in black and white. The ability to recognize shades of gray comes only with time.

I can't say this to the older people I've taught, those out of college ranging in age from their mid-twenties to late sixties. They have baggage as heavy as mine.

Some have more.

Some have baggage that's so bizarre I want to run screaming out of the classroom.

I once had the ex-wife of a notorious mobster in my screenwriting workshop. She was beautiful. Sexy. Smart. She was with him when he was assassinated. She saw him die one inch away from her. She'd only been married to him for three weeks. And her daughter by a previous marriage was there, too.

Think that her life was normal after that? And what about her daughter?

Go ahead. Top that for baggage!

George Santayana's warning not to forget the past is a caution not to make the same mistakes again.

And again.

And again.

But another good reason to remember what happened to you is the gold mine of stories lurking, sometimes deep, within your subconscious. If you're going to be a screenwriter you have to begin with a story, but where do you find the story you want to tell?

A good starting point is to look at the drama in your own life.

It's there.

Maybe not anything that happened yesterday or last week or five months ago or ten years ago, but it's in your head or your heart or buried so deep inside that maybe you've forgotten about it.

Some of that drama didn't necessarily happen to you, but you might've been indirectly affected by it.

What I'm talking about are defining moments.

My first defining moment was the death of my father when I was thirteen.

I didn't know it at the time, but that was the beginning of my baggage. Specifically, my abandonment issue. Six months after my father died my paternal grandfather died. And one month after that my favorite uncle died. My issue with loss was in full gear, although I didn't know it yet.

I have other defining moments — some good, some bad: flunking out of college my freshman year, having a gun pointed at my head for thirty-five minutes during a robbery in my apartment, *surviving* having a gun pointed at my head for thirty-five minutes during a robbery in my apartment, deciding to remain in New York rather than relocate to Los Angeles, accepting a teaching position that was supposed to last one semester and having it turn into a life-altering career change, quitting smoking, buying a dog after being a lifelong animal hater and transforming myself into an animal lover.

I have plenty more baggage, too.

So do you.

So does everybody, with time. That's why dating becomes so much more complicated as you get older. When a 15-year-old boy asks out a 14-year-old girl and it's her first date and he's maybe gone out with two other girls, they won't have much history to share.

But tag on twenty years to the same two and throw in a divorce, children, a drinking problem, depression, a business that failed, money problems, loss of hair, an addiction to pornography, and — you get the idea. Both of them will have a lot more "stuff" to work around and/or hide.

Most people are afraid to confront their baggage, let alone talk about it.

Writers not only have to drag their baggage out of the closet, but we have to relive it and analyze it and take it out to dinner. And if we're lucky, maybe we'll find the first strategy of an idea in our quest for a story.

# Writing Exercise

Grab a pen and notebook. Take a journey into your past and write down five of your defining moments; the good and the bad — *preferably* the bad.

Why?

### Your Most Interesting Experiences
### Are the Ones You'd Like to Forget

This means interesting from a dramatic point of view.

People are more interested in hearing me tell what it was like to have a gun pointed at my head for thirty-five minutes than hearing about the day I quit smoking. I consider quitting smoking one of the genuine achievements of my life, but an exciting tale it isn't.

Think about it. What's more dramatic to talk about? That horrible day off the coast of Peru when you narrowly escaped being eaten by a hammerhead shark by killing it with your bare hands or the day you found out you got that scholarship?

Both events are linchpins in your life, but only one is the kind of story you'd share around a campfire.

# Writing Exercise

As for that list of defining moments, after you've written them down, study them. Place them in their order of importance. Then try to remember how you felt when you were experiencing them. Maybe, just maybe, you'll find a launch pad for a story.

# Strategy

## Drama Doesn't Have to Be
## Life and Death to Be Life and Death

There are different levels of drama. High drama literally concerns itself with death. Someone (a princess, a president, a good person) dies tragically, suddenly, violently, young. As human beings we regularly encounter situations that aren't nearly on the level of someone dying, but are so "life and death" to our immediate peace of mind that we place tremendous energy and thought on resolving them. The dream job, dream girl, dream guy, dream house, dream agent for your screenplay. Getting revenge, getting even, getting justice, getting whatever at the right price. Satisfying a craving.

How many times in your life was your craving for a certain food so intense that you went out to get it even if it was the middle of the night or raining or snowing or — you get the idea. The point is, if you think you have to write serious dramas about big themes on life and death issues with larger-than-life characters, you're limiting yourself.

It's the small things in our lives that obsess and consume us almost daily. Those are the "life and death" dramas that are universal.

CHAPTER 6

# Give Your Protagonist a Hard Time. A *Really* Hard Time.

*"Shit happens."*
— Anonymous

Things can't go too smoothly for your main character. He has to want something, but before he gets it (*if* he gets it) he has to go through hell or at least suffer a lot.

Not a little. A lot!

Otherwise it's boring.

It's no fun watching somebody get what they want too easily. What hooks us is when we feel empathy with the hero. We like him. We want him to be happy. We identify with him. We *become* him.

But no matter how much we like him, if he doesn't suffer enough we're going to turn on him. It's like in life. If a guy is born with good looks, brains, money, charm, and athletic prowess, and also gets all the girls, is popular with men, goes to the right schools, marries into the right family, has the right connections, slides easily into a great job and seems — on the surface at least — to just sail through life, it's not interesting.

In movies, nobody roots for the rich kid. It's the under-dog that people always root for. The kid from the wrong side of the tracks with the alcoholic dad and depressed mom with zero connections and nothing but a kind heart and good soul. It's fun to watch him struggle to the top. It's no fun watching the good-looking rich kid struggle to the top because he was born there.

However — there is a way to make the rich kid a sympathetic character. Give him parents that don't love him. Make him an only child surrounded by possessions, but no love or attention — except from the maid who makes him peanut butter sandwiches after the chauffeur drives him home to an empty mansion. And give him a complex about friendship. He's convinced the only reason people like him is because he has money. And give him a stutter that makes him self-conscious. If you want to offer your readers a tragedy, give him a dark secret: He was molested by the man who cleaned the pool.

Suddenly, the rich kid has serious baggage and we feel sorry for him instead of being ambivalent about him.

He won't have the same set of obstacles and complications as the poor kid, but we'll at least be able to put aside the fact that he has money and feel sorry for him because of the negative things getting in his way. One of my students wrote a script about a nuclear bomb dropping on Manhattan. The main character was a cop, estranged from his wife and young daughter. In the course of the story the bad guy kidnaps the cop's wife and daughter, so the cop's primary goal is to find them. Finally, lo and behold, he finds them, he and his wife realize they love each other, and the family is back together.

Then the nuclear bomb is dropped. And the cop is again separated from his wife and child. End of Act II. New Information. The Exclamation Point !

It was a really nifty touch. Guy wants something, gets it, then loses it and has to get it back, only now, because of the reconciliation, it's even more important to him that he finds them. Here was the problem: his third act was only 11 pages long.

Despite his excellent **!** at the end of Act II, his choices for Act III were disastrous.

First of all, he had the cop find his wife on the next page. Then, he had them find their daughter 2 pages later. The remaining 8 pages of the script had the three of them wandering around looking for a safe place to hide.

Boring.

As I told the writer, to draw us into his story the cop had to go through one trial after another before finding his family. The cop would have to decide who he would try to find first. The writer needed to allow perhaps 10 pages for the cop to locate the wife. Then, once she's safe, he can begin his quest to find his daughter. Maybe another 15 pages. And in finding both he would have to be at great personal risk. Ultimately, with wife and daughter safe and sound, the story is over. But give it close to 30 pages, not 11.

The best movies to study for exciting third acts filled with complication after complication are action films and the best example of a state-of-the-art action flick is *Die Hard*.

I never get tired of watching it. It never gets old.

Bruce Willis is a cop who fights bad guys single-handedly. His wife is among the hostages taken by a terrorist group, and he knows the terrorists are *really* bad guys, and he loves his wife, but they've had problems, but they were going to try and reconcile, and he's willing to die for her, so he goes through hell to save her and the other hostages, and along the way there's some laughs and dramatic tension and thrills — and it works.

So by the time it's over, he's gotten what he wants and we've gotten what we want — a couple hours of escapist fun.

Same with a smaller, softer movie.

Call them what you will: complications, obstacles, roadblocks, walls — the more your character has to deal with the better your script will be.

# Strategy

## Sometimes the Structure Finds Itself

You've plotted out a solid three-act breakdown. You've begun writing the screenplay and things are rolling along smoothly, just as you planned. But then you find yourself on page 19, which in your well-planned scenario was supposed to be the end of Act I on page 30.

You have two choices: (1) Find a new event to be the end of Act I, or (2) Pad those 19 pages up so they'll stretch out to page 30. Trust me on this: padding is easier said than done. Better to let the chips, as they say, fall where they may.

Keep writing. Trust your writing.

Trust your subconscious to open a new door to go through. This can also happen when you're in Act II and Act III territory. Just as the best-laid plans of mice and men often go astray, so does the most well-prepared, clearly thought-out structure. If you've gone through two or three unexpected doors, see where they take you.

# Writing Exercise

Look at your last screenplay or the one you're working on now and make a list of the complications preventing your main character from getting what he wants. How many do you have? One? Two? Ten? The more there are, the better it is for your audience. Then look at your favorite movies and count the complications the protagonists face.

CHAPTER 7

# The Screenwriter as Jock

*"He that would perfect his work must first sharpen his tools."*

— Confucius

Once the star high school quarterback wins his scholarship to Notre Dame he keeps practicing and learning from his coaches.

And once he becomes the star college quarterback who receives national prominence and gets drafted into the pros for $15 million, he keeps practicing and learning from his coaches.

And once he becomes a star professional quarterback, he keeps practicing and learning from his coaches, as well as from all his experience.

And until the morning of the last game he plays in his professional career, he keeps practicing.

Screenwriters have to "practice" in much the same way. We have to keep writing and when we're not writing we have to be thinking things through: plot points, character motivation, dramatic peaks and valleys, act breaks, which scenes to cut, which scenes to embellish, making sure the story has a logical flow.

Just as the professional quarterback keeps working at perfecting his moves, keeping his arm free from cramps, making sure his timing is on, continually going over old plays and new plays and studying films of his opponents, screenwriters must be constantly examining and dissecting their ideas. What often makes perfect sense in your head or while you're writing it may totally fall apart when you examine it as part of the whole.

And just as every new game presents different problems and obstacles for that quarterback, every new idea, outline, treatment, and screenplay presents new problems for the screenwriter.

Not just for the screenwriter finishing a first script, but for all screenwriters, even those ten, twenty, or thirty years into their careers.

If you can't relate to sports analogies, think of the screenwriting process like dating. Every new person you go out with is different and every relationship has its own set of unique problems.

Screenwriters go through the same process. You get that vague idea, stretch it into a basic premise, then pound out the three-act breakdown.

Then you write it, all the while dodging bullets and things that don't make sense and bouncing ideas off friends and getting feedback and plowing forward until you finish the first draft.

Then start all over and do it again and again and again until you get it right.

Then you start the next one.

# Strategy

## Immediacy

Don't take too long to get the story started. Just try to have your Instigating Event happen ASAP. Page 1 is great. So is page 2 or 3. Page 4 isn't bad either. You know where I'm going with this. If you're on page 9 or 10 and you're still setting things up, you're heading for trouble.

I love it when a movie starts in the first scene... Boom! We're in it. We don't know anything about the characters or what's going on, but if it's done right, the reader and audience are hooked within seconds!

# Writing Exercise

Test your comedy writing skills by writing a *Saturday Night Live* sketch. Five pages long. Remember: A sketch is a little story with a beginning, middle, and ending. Go to *YouTube* and check out a bunch of SNL sketches. The ones that are posted are usually the best written.

CHAPTER 8

# Why Aristotle Still Matters
## (and Always Will)

*"Well begun is half done."*
— Aristotle

Aristotle lived nearly 2,400 years ago, but the ideas and theories on storytelling he set down in his *Poetics* are timelier than ever.

The six most important words Aristotle (wearing sandals and a toga) might have said to storytellers in ancient Athens are the same six words he would say to screenwriters in Hollywood today (sitting in his stretch limo, clad in Armani, sipping Evian, and making reservations at The Ivy): "Story, story, and story." Followed by "Character, character, and character."

If you never read the *Poetics* or if you haven't read them since college, they are worth taking another look. Having lectured on the *Poetics* for years, I've drawn two conclusions:

1) Brilliant as he was, Aristotle tended to overwrite and get incredibly pedantic (or perhaps the blame should go on the translators). For this reason, poring over the 40-some odd pages isn't an easy read.

2) But if you get through it, you come away with three important rules that can never be ignored.

## RULE NO. 1
## Story Is Everything

The most interesting characters "just talking" are not compelling for very long. Think of the guy who tries to tell you about the funny thing that happened on his vacation, but he rambles on and on, going off on tangents, never getting to the point.

He's lost you. And screenplays without a story, however slight, will lose their readers. Understand now that it's the people reading your screenplay that matter more than any audience, because *somebody* — an agent, producer, investor, creative executive, development person — must read your script before anything moves forward. The object is to get the person to not put down the manuscript after 15 pages, or even less.

Something must happen to the hero that propels him on a different course, either of his own doing or by having something done to him.

HIS OWN DOING

He commits an act that will have repercussions if found out. He commits a crime, cheats on his wife, drives drunk, flirts with his boss's wife, bets the mortgage money on a horse race.

SOMETHING DONE TO HIM

He is the innocent victim of someone else's actions: his wife is murdered and he's accused, he's unjustifiably fired, his teenage daughter is kidnapped.

## RULE NO. 2
## The Story Must Start at the Right Time

Specifically, not too late. The earlier the better. Don't take forty pages to establish who your character is and what situation he finds himself in. In a novel (and to a lesser extent, a play) you can ease into plot and character. In a screenplay you can't.

## RULE NO. 3
### Keep the Line of Dramatic Action Moving

This is where plot and complications come in. Plot is the placement of dramatic incidents. This happens, then that happens, then this, then that, then....

Complications are the things that get in the hero's way. They shouldn't be insurmountable, but don't make them a breeze to overcome.

It's like dating. There is a man waiting in line at a bank. The woman in front of him is attractive. The man might say, "Hi. You're cute. I love you. Want to get married?" And she might say, "Okay. There's a justice-of-the-peace around the corner. Let's go."

The story's over. It lasted barely ten seconds. There was no challenge for the hero and nothing compelling for the audience to care about or root for or root against.

But if the situation were more realistic: same man, same woman, same line, same bank. The man starts up a conversation. The woman ignores him. He persists. She tells him to buzz off. He tries one more time. This time she's had it and says, "I could never go out with you because you look like the man I hate most in the world."

Now we have a story. Turns out the man loves a challenge (which in itself is a good character attribute), so despite the woman's honesty he will attempt to overcome all obstacles and win her heart.

And to really make it interesting, after he finally does win her heart and undying devotion, then he doesn't want her. Now she wants him.

And to make it even more compelling, she's psychotic and has a history of tormenting men who reject her.

And to make this script even more of a page-turner, the man has an "issue" about being pursued by women, so the harder she chases him, the more he's turned off.

By the time all these twists and turns have occurred, we like these people. Both are damaged and because we've spent 100 pages with them we've come to care about them despite their foibles and neurosis. We just know they'd be perfect for each other (with some couple therapy), so as we read the final pages we're sincerely hoping they get together.

And on the last page of the script, they do.

And we're satisfied.

That's a story.

# Strategy

## The Ending in the Beginning

If you can conceal the ending of your screenplay in its beginning, you are pulling off something magical. Sometimes we'll be totally into a film, not sure how it's going to end, having our own theories or hopes, and then we're surprised. It ended in a manner we never suspected, but then after thinking about it, we realize that the hints were there all along, some from the opening scenes. Check out *Shutter Island* as a fine example of this. *The Sixth Sense*, too.

Fool me until I'm on the last page of your screenplay and you've done your job as a screenwriter. I know how most screenplays and movies are going to end simply because I see things coming. My guess is that a lot of moviegoers of all ages are like this too. Character behavior and plots that are predictable quickly become boring. All the fun is taken away and you start to regret dishing out that ever-increasing price of admission. People love being fooled and surprised when things go unexpectedly in a different direction. This is even more important in a screenplay. You overcome a gigantic hurdle by keeping agents, producers, and development executives guessing until the final Fade Out.

# Writing Exercise

Write a character history of the main character of the screenplay you're writing now, the one you just finished, or the one you're about to start. What should it contain? Anything you already know about the character. If you don't know much other than his name, then use this opportunity to figure out exactly who this person is.

I've read character histories that were extremely detailed, starting with something that happened to the character at the age of three, and others that listed only the character's interests and flaws. Every writer does it differently. Make your history as long or short as you choose.

CHAPTER 9

# Is Your Idea Big Enough to Go the Distance?

*"All good ideas arrive by chance."*
— Max Ernst

Prose writers go through this all the time. Is the idea a short story, novella, short novel, or full-blown novel? Playwrights must decide if their new idea is a ten-minute play, short one act (15 to 30 pages), long one act (30 to 60 pages) or a full-length two- or three-act play?

Screenwriters are in the same boat and it's a less flexible boat. Is it a short screenplay or full length? And unless you're a film student in a class where your assignment is to make a short film (usually anywhere from five to twenty-five minutes), there isn't much of a call for short scripts like these.

The only other reason to write a short screenplay is that you plan to direct it as a showcase for yourself. The fact is that most new screenwriters — though the possibility of directing looms as something for the future — are mainly concerned with writing a full-length screenplay.

This is where important decisions have to be made.

Is your idea big enough to sustain interest for 110 pages or even 100 pages? What do I mean by "big enough"? Consider the various movies inspired by sketches that originated on

*Saturday Night Live*. Most didn't work because what is hilarious in five- to seven-minute sketches seen a bunch of times over two or three seasons is difficult to translate into a long form storyline that is as consistently funny.

"Less is more" clearly applies. Not that all the *Saturday Night Live* spinoffs didn't work. *The Blues Brothers* and *Wayne's World* did. But *MacGruber*, *Superstar*, and *The Ladies Man* didn't. The *Coneheads* missed and *A Night At The Roxbury* was entertaining, although it petered out near the end.

The best way to gauge what length your script should be is to use the song test. Most early rock songs came in around 3 minutes due to the limitations of the 45 rpm format. But some of the greatest hits from rock's Golden Era were unusually long or uniquely short. The Animal's 1964 version of *The House of the Rising Sun* was the first rock hit over 4 minutes. Once enabled by the LP (long-playing) record, artists could produce such '60s classics as *MacArthur's Park* (Richard Harris) and *You Can't Always Get What You Want* (The Rolling Stones), each over 7 minutes long. While Lennon and McCartney's jewel of a song, *I Will*, was a mere 1 minute and 47 seconds.

Long or short, these songs were successful because they were the length they *needed* to be to work. The same applies with your screenplay. If you can successfully tell your story in 102 pages, that's what it needs to be and you're done. If you need 120 pages to tell your story, so be it. You're done (and you've passed the song test).

All things being equal, if you have a hunch that your idea isn't big enough or if you start working on it and your gut feeling is that it's not sustainable for a hundred pages, you have two options: find a strong subplot or have the courage to junk the idea until you *can* find a subplot.

# Strategy

Length is a major problem for all screenwriters. You're either an over-writer or an under-writer. I'm not talking about people who finish scripts that come in at 168 pages (way too long) or 83 pages (way too short). Those are entirely different problems. I mean scripts that should be cut or embellished by only a few pages.

There is a trick that helps. If you have a CUT TO after every scene in your overlong screenplay, to trim it down simply eliminate each CUT TO. On the other hand, if you didn't use CUT TOs in your 98-page script, to bulk it up you should add them. The use of CUT TO between scenes is redundant anyway, because once a scene ends, it is understood that the next scene is "cut to."

# Writing Exercise

Conflict is possibly the most difficult aspect of writing for writers to grasp. You can't just have people talking. There should be something at stake. One person wants something and must persuade the other person to give it to him. To make it interesting, the other person doesn't *want* to give it to him.

This is called reciprocal action. Practice writing two-character scenes in which each character refuses to budge.

CHAPTER 10

# Before You Can See the World, You Have to Get to the Airport

*"Who so neglects learning in his youth loses the past and is dead for the future."*

— Euripides

Drunk frat boys notwithstanding, it's fair to assume that most people don't just decide on pure whim to drop what they're doing, jump in the car, and take a 3,000-mile cross-country trip.

If a trip or vacation is going to be taken, there's usually some semblance of a plan.

We're going to drive from New York to Los Angeles and along the way stop in Pittsburg, Kansas, to visit Aunt Grace; then we're stopping in Phoenix to see Uncle Hank and, if there is time, we're going to take a detour and visit Yellowstone National Park.

That's the plan. You know where you're going. You've given yourself an estimated time frame, budgeted your money — and if you're really responsible — made reservations in motels.

Structuring a plot should be handled in the same way.

It isn't wise to just sit down and start writing without even the remotest thread of a plot. Even the barest semblance of a plan will help.

In television they call it the "Premise" (or Logline), usually a catchy sentence describing the episode of a particular show: In this week's episode of *30 Rock*, the guy who ruined Liz Lemon's senior prom shows up to make amends, and against her better judgment, she starts dating him again. It's clear enough to give us an idea of the nature of the episode.

Think of this sentence as:

## THE VAGUE IDEA

The Vague Idea is the slim notion of a story that tweaks your imagination. The following examples are from Steven Spielberg movies: *Jaws, E. T.,* and *Saving Private Ryan*, plus one original created by me, entitled *Smothered with Onions*.

- A great white shark terrorizes a town.

- An alien child is left behind on Earth and must find a way to get home.

- After surviving World War II's D-Day invasion, eight American soldiers must go behind enemy lines to find a GI and bring him back safely.

- A modest, low-key chef loses his job because of his lack of personal flamboyance, so he reinvents himself.

Next comes the expansion of the vague idea into a:

## BASIC PREMISE

This may be only a few sentences that help to clarify where the story might go. Remember: You haven't written a word of the script yet. You're just thinking at this point.

### Expansion of the Vague Idea of *Jaws* Into a Basic Premise

A great white shark terrorizes a *beach* town during the *lucrative Fourth of July weekend*. (Suddenly, the stakes are raised. If the town, which relies heavily on summer tourist trade, lets it be known that a great white shark is in the water, the town and its small businesses risk financial ruin.) More expansion: Two people are killed. A shark expert who is called in says the predator isn't just "a shark" but a great white. The beaches must be closed, but the town and local businesses still have to worry about financial ruin, so an eccentric local fisherman is hired to find and kill the great white. Helping him is the police chief and the shark expert. In the course of the story the three form an odd bond and eventually kill the shark.

This expansion tells us more about the story. The next step is to expand it into a three-act outline or breakdown. This is the hard part.

It forces you to think your idea through to the point where it's no longer a vague idea, but a larger premise and a fuller concept.

Here's an exercise to force yourself to think beyond that vague idea, through the basic premise, and into a fairly well thought-out storyline.

A guy meets this girl and they get together. (Way too vague.)

A guy meets this girl he used to know. (Not much better.)

A guy meets this girl he used to know in high school who played a hurtful prank on him with her girlfriends that made him mistrustful of women. (Getting closer.)

Let's pump up the volume a bit:

A guy meets the girl he had a crush on in high school, but she wouldn't give him the time of day then because he was the geeky, creepy son of a mortician and she was the head cheerleader and wouldn't be caught dead even talking to him. (Longer and still vague, but we're heading toward something.)

A guy who used to be nerdy in high school, but is now handsome and rich, crosses paths with the girl he loved in high school. But he doesn't recognize her: she has now lost her looks, weighs two-hundred pounds, has bad hair, bad skin, and needs a kidney transplant, and works the late shift at a factory where she lost a finger in a freak accident. When the guy buys the factory, he realizes that this woman is the girl he once loved. And the thing is, he *still loves her.* All his success meant nothing, so he decides to try again. But she *still thinks he's a geek* and still rejects him. He decides to try to win her over.

That is by no means a vague idea. And it's stronger than a basic premise. And there's enough plot in that long paragraph to give a sense of where the story will go.

The next step is to write the three-act storyline. But before getting to the storyline it's important to point out that the hardest part of writing the storyline is pinpointing how the story will end.

You have to come up with an ending to something you haven't even begun writing yet, something you haven't even thought about other than a momentary surge of inspiration. It's like trying to figure out on Monday morning what you want for dessert at dinner on Friday night.

The only way to accomplish this is by pushing yourself to think things through.

It's a bitch to do this, but it can be done. And once you know how, you're closer to having a destination. And the destination is to know how your story is going to end.

Even in the storyline I just created, what's missing is how it will end. I don't know yet for sure. Will he win her over? Will he pursue her and help her get her life back in order? Will she fall for him?

This is the hard part. I'm like the drunken frat boys who find themselves in the middle of nowhere without money, credit cards, gasoline, a map, or a plan.

And this is where the work begins.

# Writing Exercise

As a simple exercise, *you* end my story. But give me three endings. One happy. One sad. One dark.

Why three possible endings? Each will be different and will create its own unique tone that will affect your thinking when you actually begin writing the screenplay.

If in the dark ending you know the main character will die, you'll write the script one way. If you know the woman will die in his arms and that he'll be devastated, you'll write the script another way. If it's a big Hollywood ending, you'll write it in yet another way.

But above all else, through this tiny collaboration of ours, we will have a beginning, a middle, and an end.

We will have a map for the 115-or-so page journey that we would take if we were going to actually write the screenplay.

In the next chapter you'll see how I took my vague idea for a play titled *Smothered with Onions* and expanded it into a three-act outline.

# Strategy

## Lost in Pennsylvania

From my apartment in New York City to my mother's home in Northeastern Ohio, door-to-door, it's a ten-hour drive. That breaks down like this: two hours through New Jersey to the Pennsylvania border, six-and-a-half hours through Pennsylvania to the Ohio border, and another ninety minutes to my mother's house.

This ten-hour drive pretty much reflects how a screenplay is structured. I came up with this little theory the first time I made the drive and got momentarily lost in the middle of Pennsylvania.

I mention this simply because I was working on a screenplay at the time and I had hit a wall. Remember how I had counseled the young writer that to draw us into his story, the cop hero had to go through one trial after another before finding his family? It would probably take the writer 10 pages to have his hero locate his wife, another 10 to have him locate his daughter, and the hero would have to be at great personal risk on page 55 — roughly the middle of the second act.

Most of my students hit a wall in the middle of the second act. I came to describe this phenomenon as being lost in Pennsylvania. It *will* happen.

There *will* be a wall.

You *will* find a way to break through it.

CHAPTER 11

# The Importance of Outlines

*"If you don't know where you're going you will wind up somewhere else."*

— Dr. Laurence Peter, *The Peter Principle*

Having a destination is important in creating a successful outline. The vaguest ideas and the most expanded premises mean nothing unless your storyline arrives at its destination and ends with a resolution. Pinpointing the resolution at this early stage is where most screenwriters have problems.

"How can I know how it will end before I even start writing?" is the most common refrain.

The answer is to force yourself to come up with a probable resolution to the story, if for no other reason than to give yourself a destination.

It's like those previously mentioned frat boys who take off on the cross-country trip without ten seconds of preparation versus the frat boys who plan their junket. The guys with money, gas, clothing, places to stay, and a map are better suited for travel than the others.

Neither set of frat boys may get to where they're going as planned, just like you may wind up in a different — and better — place than your storyline indicated. But to write blindly without any sense of where you're going is just as foolhardy as jumping in your car at three in the morning and going somewhere.

The following takes you step-by-step through the process of defining the initial vague idea, expanding it into the basic premise, then spreading it out into a three-act outline (or breakdown) with a beginning, middle, and end.

### Smothered with Onions
### Written by
### D. B. Gilles

## VAGUE IDEA
Modest, low-key chef loses his job because of his lack of charisma, so he reinvents himself.

## BASIC PREMISE
Modest, low-key chef loses his job at an exclusive restaurant because of his lack of charisma and unimaginative recipes. To save his career, he decides to reinvent himself as a flashy, 300-pound, bigger-than-life chef from the Southwest with colorful, fattening regional dishes.

He becomes a superstar chef, best-selling author, and host of his own show on the Food Network. But his new-found success and wealth prove unsatisfactory because he's not being true to himself and he's fallen for a woman who's in love with his reinvented self.

### ACT I
Open by introducing RANDY DUFORE, late twenties, the chef of a struggling Los Angeles restaurant specializing in French peasant cooking. Business is slipping and the owner fires Randy for the simple reason that it's the era of the dashing celebrity chefs with flamboyant personalities and colorful takes on different cuisines. (Instigating Event)

Randy is devastated. His credentials are impeccable. He studied at Le Cordon Bleu in Paris and apprenticed at three major American restaurants.

But the one thing he lacks is flair. That can't be taught. (Question: What will happen to Randy's career as a chef?)

He licks his wounds by going back to his hometown in Oklahoma. He spends time with the person who got him interested in cooking in the first place: his grandmother, who raised him. She still runs the small restaurant where Randy cut his teeth. We learn that, despite Randy's fine education in Continental cuisine, his roots are in down-home Southwestern food. We also find out that he is more than a little ashamed of where he comes from.

Randy and his grandmother have a soul-searching talk in which she says that every chef has to find his niche. If one cuisine doesn't click, find another. If that doesn't work, keep looking until you find what works, then stay with it.

Before returning to Los Angeles, Randy has lunch at a small roadhouse diner where he observes a wisecracking, overweight Mexican short-order cook with a huge handlebar mustache regaling his customers as he serves up fattening, delectable Southwestern/Tex-Mex dishes.

Inspiration strikes. Randy models himself after the Mexican cook, goes back to Los Angeles, hires an acting coach, resurrects the Southern accent he spent years trying to lose, dons a wig, grows a handlebar mustache, and, through padding, makes himself appear to weigh 300 pounds.

He then presents himself as TUCKER LEE PETTI-BONE.

Using the many down-home recipes he learned as a boy from his grandmother, he sets out to start a new career. (Major Dramatic Question: Will he pull it off?) **?**

## ACT II

After a few minor setbacks, largely due to his inability to stay in the "Tucker Lee" character, he gets a job. The restaurant is a success and so is "Tucker." While Randy would stay in the kitchen at the restaurant he was fired from, "Tucker" works the room. Everybody loves him.

And sure enough, things take off. His flamboyance gets him a deal for a cookbook, then his own cooking show on the Food Network.

Things go great for him, except for two things: He falls in love with a woman who digs fat men, and so he has to pretend he's this hugely overweight fellow all the time. (Complication) This presents problems when it comes to sex. A subplot deals with the woman trying to get him in bed and him constantly finding ways to avoid getting naked in front of her, thus exposing that he isn't really who he says he is. (Complication)

In one scene, without his "fat" disguise, Randy attempts to make conversation with the woman, but because he's thin and low-key, she's not interested. So Randy knows that to be with her he has to play Tucker Lee Pettibone to the hilt. (Complication)

As fame and fortune come, his ego gets the better of him and he wants the world to know who he really is. But he's afraid that the "real" person won't be as accepted as his dynamic alter ego and he's even more concerned that the woman won't be interested in his "thin and trim" self.

So Randy is forced to live life as a fraud, and a fat fraud at that. (Complication)

To further complicate things, a snobbish female food critic begins to suspect that Tucker Lee Pettibone isn't for real. (Major complication and Middle of Act II event) Since Randy has fabricated an entire backstory for "Tucker," when the food critic tries to verify some of his biographical data she comes up blank. She then sets out to discover just who Tucker Lee Pettibone really is.

The critic ultimately discovers the truth and confronts Randy. She decides to blackmail him. She'll keep his secret in exchange for a piece of the action in his new restaurant, as well as a percentage of his cookbook royalties.

If he doesn't agree, she'll go public and expose him.

(New Information that propels us into Act III.) **!**

## ACT III

Randy has reached a turning point. He's so frustrated from pretending to be Tucker Lee that he's almost relieved the jig is up. But what's tearing him apart is the fact that the woman he's crazy about (who is turned on by fat men) won't be interested in him when she finds out that he's really thin — and that he lied.

He decides to come clean with the truth during a live broadcast of his cooking show on the Food Network.

He does so. (Obligatory Scene)

And he reverts back to his humble, subdued self.

To his surprise, he's accepted by his fans. Turns out that the popularity of the arrogant, egomaniacal chef prototype is fading fast and the more down-to-earth type is becoming desirable. More importantly, he accepts the fact that while he may have disguised who he was, *the recipes are his!* We'll have seen that he combined his French training with his grandmother's recipes to create sensational meals.

As far as the girl who likes fat men, she drops him, but the producer of his cooking show (who has always had a crush on him) and he get together. **.**

### The End†

This is now beyond the vague idea and basic premise. After reading this outline, you can see where the story will go once it's time to start writing the script.

For some screenwriters, this is enough. For others, there's still more to do. You probably won't know which category you'll fall into until you've tried to write a full treatment. In my experience, people either like doing them or hate the process.

---

†Registered, WGA, East

If you're the kind of screenwriter who finds comfort in thinking things through and knowing exactly where your storyline is going before plowing into the screenplay, the next step is to write a full scale treatment ranging in length from 15 to 25 pages.

If the three-act outline for *Smothered with Onions* is detailed enough to give you an idea of where the screenplay will go, imagine how detailed a 15 or 20 page treatment would be. Besides the narrative of the story, dialogue would be included, characters would be better defined, and subplots expanded, eliminated, or reduced.

I can't emphasize this enough: long treatments aren't for everyone, but I feel adamantly that everyone should do a three-act outline. To just "start writing" is folly. And as Dr. Laurence Peter decreed, "If you don't know where you're going you will wind up somewhere else."

# Writing Exercise

Following this format, write a three-act outline of the next screenplay you intend to write. Create strong end-moments for your first and second acts.

# Strategy

## The Heat That Melts Butter Hardens Steel

This Yiddish saying helps to make sense of why the same tragedy affects people differently. There's a terrible car accident involving two friends. Both survive, but are paraplegics. One is filled with rage, turns bitter, and hates being alive. The other is grateful to be alive, learns to appreciate all the things he can do, and rolls with the punches. Either way, here is the beginning of the creation of one character or another, and either would be interesting.

One woman who is raped is shamed by the assault, tells no one, keeps it to herself, and tries to live as if nothing is wrong. Another rape victim becomes empowered, is unashamed, confronts her attacker, presses charges, bravely takes him to court, and sees justice through. Stories are to be found in the way people handle the cards they are dealt.

# CHAPTER 12

# Eccentrics, or How That 7-Eleven Clerk with the Bad Eye Can Make Your Script Better

*"Now, here, you see, it takes all the running you can do to keep in the same place."*

> — Lewis Carroll
> *Through the Looking Glass*

The best stories are often about outcasts, eccentrics, misfits, and people who aren't in the mainstream of life.

You know who they are. The woman who never marries and becomes a companion to her mother because her father is either dead, inattentive, or a drunk. Or maybe she's afraid to leave mom because she's been warned ad nauseam that men are bastards, so to protect herself from being hurt like her mother was, she remains close to the hearth.

Then there's the son who got married and divorced and came back home and now just sticks around. He gains weight, takes care of his folks, looks after his brother who has Down syndrome, or tries to make a go of the struggling family business.

The sister and brother who steer clear of marriage manage to leave home, but avoid independence by becoming roommates. They rent until they're in their thirties, when — as middle age looms ahead, dates become less frequent, and security becomes a new factor — they buy a place together and live platonically as a couple.

Have you ever wondered about the late-night clerk at the 7-Eleven with the weird overbite and bad eye? He dates the chubby girl with the mole on the tip of her nose who works the graveyard shift at the donut factory. How about the religious 40-year-old woman in the church choir who is so pathologically shy she can't talk to anyone, especially men. (The exception is priests, whom she adores because her own father was so emotionally distant and, of course, being priests, they are safe.) Or consider the lifer at the company, married to his job, whose personal life is so empty he goes into the office on weekends but doesn't put in for overtime.

You know who I'm talking about. They're everywhere. Every family has at least one. Weird Uncle George who does odd jobs at a funeral home, coaches little league, lives in an apartment over a friend's garage, and goes to science fiction conventions. Creepy Aunt Bonnie who quotes scripture and secretly downs a fifth of Jack Daniel's every night and calls in to local radio talk shows. Cousin Bert who doesn't know he's gay.

And, of course, there are the people who are literally and physically out of the mainstream of life, the homeless. The homeless person who interests me as a writer and student of human behavior is the one who is intelligent, cunning. The one who had the big job. Who made the big bucks. Who had the house in the suburbs and all its responsibilities. Why is this guy on the street?

In fact, a great film has already been made on this subject, *The Fisher King* (1991) with Robin Williams. If you can't find an idea to get excited about or a character that interests you, look at the outcasts, eccentrics, and lost souls around you, not judgmentally, but with curiosity and compassion. They're human beings too, but they live their lives way off the beaten path. If you have the courage to go down that path you may find an incredible story to write.

# Writing Exercise

Make a list of five oddball characters you encounter on a regular basis. Create a character history for each one. Imagine what happened in their lives that made them the way they are (or how you perceive them to be).

# Strategy

## Just Because It Really Happened Doesn't Mean It Belongs in Your Screenplay

Some people have no problem coming up with ideas to write about. Others have a difficult time finding any, so they make the mistake of writing about things that really happened to them.

It's one thing to write a movie based on the camping trip your family took when you were fifteen and your parents bonded with you and your brother and everyone returned home closer than ever. But if you write a script chronicling every moment the way it actually happened, you aren't writing a screenplay, you're making a documentary.

A screenplay is fiction, an invention. Maybe inspired by some real life event, but largely made up. Go ahead and let that long-ago camping trip be the catalyst of a story, but add dramatic spice by having an escaped convict show up and kidnap your mother. That way, you, your brother and father can bond while trying to save mom. I'm a firm believer that writers should write what they know. But being a writer means using your imagination to enhance and expand what you know.

If you want to chronicle real events the way they happened, don't write screenplays. Make documentaries.

# Writing Exercise

Write the vague ideas that inspired the last three screenplays you wrote. If you're about to start your first screenplay, write your vague idea for it. It may take some time. They're not easy, even for experienced screenwriters. After you've written the vague ideas, refine them. Make them compelling. Bounce them off one or two of your friends. See what they think. Then look at what you wrote again. Keep refining and streamlining them until you know your vague idea rocks.

CHAPTER 13

# The Weenie Surprise and the "Now What?" Factor

*"Knowledge must come through action; you can have no test which is not fanciful, save by trial."*

— Sophocles

Making it through Acts I and II are major victories, but most screenplays run into trouble in Act III. This happens because in constructing the story, a screenwriter fails to keep building the dramatic tension in Act II to carry the reader to the next high point of the story.

As discussed earlier, think of Act II as 50 to 60 pages of complications, twists, turns, and wrinkles, all building to an event that gives the reader an **!** or *new information*.

Ideally, this new information should come as a complete surprise to the reader, something totally unexpected. Info that literally causes the reader to smile, guffaw, or twitch from the shock of being fooled.

The best example of a second act ending that I've ever seen is from the 1992 Neil Jordan film *The Crying Game*.

The new information he provided his audience with has to do with what I call...

### The Weenie Surprise

An IRA splinter group has kidnapped a British soldier. A reluctant member of the group assigned to watch the prisoner befriends him. The prisoner carries on about his girlfriend in London, how badly he wants to be with her. But the prisoner is killed and the reluctant terrorist feels compelled to visit the girl in London and tell her of her boyfriend's death.

Only problem is, the terrorist falls in love with the girl who is a singer in a nightclub.

As we build to the end of Act II, the terrorist finds out that the girl is really a *guy*. We discover this when the two of them are about to make love for the first time.

We see the girl/guy's penis. Yikes! That's what I call new information.

The beauty of this powerful moment is that it gives the main character a moral dilemma to deal with for the rest of the story: despite the fact that *he* is straight, he has come to love the girl/guy.

So what does he do?

If you haven't seen the film, I've spoiled the surprise at the end of Act II, but I won't spoil the third act for you because the screenwriter fills it with enough additional twists and turns to culminate in a brilliantly satisfying ending.

Needless to say, this is an extreme example of a powerful end moment of Act II. I believe we never forget the best examples *because* they are extreme.

Previously I dealt with the mathematics of structure. The end of Act I should come on or about page 30, the end of Act II should come around page 82 to 90 (depending upon the length of your script), and Act III should wrap up about page 115 to 120.

Never forget that as you're heading toward the end of Act II that you must give us a big event/twist/surprise/reversal/piece of new information that will hook us and make us turn the pages to find out what's going to happen.

But what do you do if your story isn't sensational or outrageous and you can't rely on the appearance of an unexpected male organ?

No problem.

You have to use what I call...

### The "Now What?" Factor

A terrific example of this is found in *The Secret in Their Eyes*, winner of the Academy Award in 2009 for Best Foreign Film.

The story, set in 1999, is told in flashback. In June, 1974, an Argentinean federal justice agent, Benjamín Espósito, becomes involved in the investigation of a young woman's rape and murder. (Instigating Event) The victim's husband, Ricardo Morales, is devastated and Espósito vows to bring the killer to justice. The grieving husband elaborates on what justice means to him, saying that a death sentence for the killer is too easy. A lonely life sentence in prison for the killer would be better revenge.

Espósito is helped by his assistant, Pablo Sandoval, and the new department chief, an Ivy League–educated lawyer named Irene Menéndez-Hastings. Espósito's rival agent, Romano, pins the murder on two innocent construction workers to quickly close the case.

But Espósito persists, finding a clue in some old pictures provided by the victim's husband. There is a young man in the photographs, Isidoro Gómez, who in each shot seems to be gazing at the future victim in a suspicious way.

In search of Gómez, Espósito and Sandoval break into Gómez' mother's home in the city where both Gómez and the victim once lived. The investigator and his assistant obtain letters written by the suspect to his mother, but neither can make anything out of the letters. By sheer luck, Sandoval comes across a new lead: A fellow drinker in his local bar identifies the names mentioned in the letters as being those of players on a Buenos Aires soccer team.

Espósito and Sandoval attend a soccer match in vague hopes of catching Gómez, which, surprisingly, they do. Espósito and department chief Hastings interrogate Gómez, who eventually confesses to the murder. Justice seems elusive, however, as barely a year later Gómez is given an early release.

End of Act II.

So where's the new information? What about the Weenie Surprise?

Actually, most scriptwriters don't build to something as outrageous as a drag queen to tweak their audience. So the next best thing is to give them a powerful moment or event that will grab them emotionally and make them say, "Now what?"

The "Now what?" at the end of Act II of *The Secret in Their Eyes* is asked now that the killer is free. Justice has not been served. "Now what" will the main character do?

So we're into Act III. But the beauty of the film is that there's another "Now what?" moment.

The story returns to 1999. Espósito has an uneventful career in Buenos Aires until his retirement. Haunted by the past, he's determined to write down his story in novel form. He drives to meet Morales, the murder victim's husband, who now lives a quiet life in the country. There, a hesitant Morales confesses to having lured Gómez to a remote spot and executing him back in 1975, soon after the murderer was released.

Cool! Wow! Nobody expected that piece of information. Okay. "Now what?"

A disturbed Espósito leaves, but upon mulling over certain facts, secretly returns to Morales' house. Sneaking inside, he is shocked to find that Morales has a makeshift prison cell in his home. There, he has kept Gómez *chained inside for over 24 years* to punish him for raping, then killing his wife.

Even cooler! More new information. "Now what?"

Morales has kept the killer alive by feeding him and tending to him, but not once in 24 years has he spoken to him nor let him out of the confining cell. Morales repeats what he had said to Espósito back to 1974: that, instead of a death sentence for the killer, a meaningless life in a cage would be the harshest justice.

Now, the major dramatic question has been finally answered. Knowing that Gómez will never be a free man again, Espósito finally comes to terms with his own life.

Never forget that an audience is willing to go along with you to the very end as long as you keep offering surprises. Some screenplays fascinate readers from the opening scene. Others take their time and seduce them slowly through several scenes after which readers are mesmerized. But the very best screenplays grab us, demand our every breath of attention, then release us — exhausted, drenched — on the final page.

# Strategy

## A Lesson from Chili about Feedback

One of my hobbies is cooking and one of my best recipes is chili. Chili was also one of the first things I learned to make when the cooking bug hit me.

I started by following my mother's recipe. It was pretty basic. Ground meat, kidney beans, an onion, couple of bacon strips, can of tomatoes, and some chili powder.

That became my recipe. For a while. The problem was that I liked my chili spicy. I checked out a few cooking shows on public TV and looked through some cookbooks, one in particular called *Chili Madness*, which contains a diverse selection of chili recipes.

Somewhere along the line I heard about this seasoning called cumin. And somebody else told me about the value of jalapeño peppers. Somewhere else I picked up the idea of throwing in Hershey's Cocoa, not for flavoring, but for looks; it added darkness to the meat. And then came the dash of vinegar. And following that the pinch of sugar.

Then I heard about the theory that dark kidney beans were preferable to light. My Aunt Grace liked to use one can of dark and one can of pink for a more artistic presentation.

Along the way I also picked up the thesis that the kidney beans shouldn't be put in the pot until moments before serving. Somebody else used garlic. Lots of people, especially from Texas, think it's sacrilegious to use beans. Somebody else refuses to use ground meat and will only use chunks of beef.

Cilantro can be controversial, too. When do you put it in? Too soon and it loses its taste. Too late and it can dominate. Then it gets crazy. Some people put in a can of beer. Others serve their chili with mashed potatoes. Others still with spaghetti.

The point of all this is to re-emphasize the value of feedback and criticism. You write an outline or treatment or first draft and you're alone. Is it good or bad or mediocre or what? Is it worth continuing? Is it too much like something else? Is it a winner?

You talk it out with someone. Bounce it off a couple of others. Or you let someone read what you've written.

While I'm not a believer in brutal criticism, I do believe in being honest. Nobody learns anything from a critic who is kind and, well, polite. But I don't believe people learn anything from harsh vitriol, either.

The way to benefit from feedback is to be selective in who you show your work to. Just as I learned to be particular about whose ingredients I borrowed for my chili recipe, I've learned to be choosy about whose criticism I accept and reject. My family never sees anything. Ever. They love me and they've always been too kind. Being too kind is almost as bad as being too honest. I've heard criticism given under the guise of "being honest" that was so pitiless it made me sick to my stomach.

I've been able to find a few people who will acknowledge what works and what doesn't work. Hearing what works is fine, but what I'm most interested in is what doesn't. And if I'm really lucky, someone will have suggestions to help fix whatever the problems might be.

I consider all the feedback and suggestions, accept or reject what feels right, then I get to work. It's still my screenplay, even if I utilized the suggestions and feedback or even lines of dialogue.

Just like my recipe for chili — despite the ingredient suggestions, it's still my chili.

# Writing Exercise

Re-watch — or, better yet, read the screenplays of — your five favorite movies. Then, for each film, pinpoint the instigating event, introduction of the major dramatic question, end-of-Act I moment, introduction of the subplot, middle-of-Act II event, end-of-Act II event, and the moment the major dramatic question is answered.

CHAPTER 14

# The Case of the Missing Third Act, or Is It Over Already?

*"Always be closing."*
— Salesman's Motto

Sometimes a script can build to a terrific end of Act II only to crash and burn in Act III.

The problem is that the major dramatic question of the story is resolved too quickly. A perfect example of this is an obscure film from 1991 called *Late for Dinner*.

I want to state up front that I loved this movie, but only until a certain point. Here's the premise:

In 1962, two guys get themselves cryogenically frozen for what should be one night, but due to some major complications, it turns into twenty-nine years.

The main character, Willie, is twenty-five, married, and has an infant daughter. So when he and his pal wake up twenty-nine years later, he's *still* twenty-five, but his beloved wife, Joy, is pushing fifty-five and his young daughter is older than he was when he "left."

We learn that both mother and daughter always assumed Willie took off and abandoned them back in 1962. They went on with their lives.

The plot boils down to Willie finding a way to convince his wife and daughter that he has indeed returned after being frozen for twenty-nine years.

As goofy as this sounds, the execution worked. After suspending your disbelief, you go with it and you root for Willie to somehow convince these adult women that it's really him.

There are plenty of complications and twists along the way, but the story builds nicely to the big moment when the 25-year-old hero *finally* convinces the 55-year-old Joy (who looks more like his mother than the young woman he married twenty-nine years ago) that he is indeed who he says he is.

They kiss. It's very moving and touching.

I said to myself, "A perfect way to end Act II."

But guess what? As they're kissing, the credits start to roll. The movie is over. I felt cheated.

To me, the *real* story was just beginning, namely: How will this couple, once very much in love when they were both young, get along now after all this time? Joy has twenty-nine years of life experience on Willie. He's still twenty-five and he hasn't the slightest idea about the major changes in society while he was frozen, let alone the changes that certainly occurred in his wife.

To me, the third act should have dealt with the problems this couple would realistically have faced.

That would have been dramatic and satisfying.

Instead, I left the theater unsatisfied and ticked off at the screenwriters.

But sometimes you see a movie that ends abruptly and doesn't necessarily tie up loose ends, yet leaves you strangely satisfied and wanting nothing.

This approach to screenwriting might be described like this:

## It Has a Nice Beat and You Can Dance to It

A film that exemplifies this beautifully is *The Full Monty.*

Two unemployed, down-on-their-luck British working class guys observe how the local women spend money to watch some Chippendale-like dancers strip down to their drawers. They get the idea to put on a similar show with the exception that they will drop their drawers completely (referred to in Britain as showing "the full Monty"). These two set out to find a few others to join them, and despite personal problems in their own lives, eventually rent a pub, dance, and drop their drawers.

The End. Fini. That's all folks.

Any way you look at it, it's over.

The writer had his characters do what he said they would do.

We didn't follow up on what happened to the protagonists or if they were going to be alright or if the one guy would get back with his wife or if the other would get custody of his child or anything.

It just *ended* and millions of people the world over walked out of the theater satisfied.

And believe me, if you haven't seen the movie, it ended quite unexpectedly, with a freeze-frame rear shot of the five naked guys.

It ended just as abruptly as *Late for Dinner,* but *The Full Monty* worked.

The plot was simple and clear. The heroes were very human. Regular guys. None of them pretty boys. One is fat. They were all in bad places in their lives and they weren't that young. Regular folks the world over identified with these guys.

It wasn't *Citizen Kane* or *Schindler's List* or *Dr. Zhivago* or *Raging Bull* or anywhere near a great film or a great script. It was, well, it was sweet. And nice. And fun.

And like the kids used to say long ago on American Bandstand, "It has a nice beat and you can dance to it."

*Late for Dinner* was too hard to dance to. Another problem was that *Late for Dinner* didn't set the tone it was going to follow early on.

Setting the tone is another way of setting the rules of a game.

*Late for Dinner* presented itself as a high-concept love story. It failed because it thought the concept would carry the day, when in reality in love stories it's the romance that people remember.

Think fast! What was the plot of *Casablanca*? Unless it tripped off your tongue you don't remember. But I bet you remember the love story. Bogart is running a bar and his life is turned upside down when Ingrid Bergman, the lost love of his life, walks in. "Of *all* the gin joints, in *all* the towns, in *all* the world, she walks into mine," he says. From that moment on, all we care about is whether or not they'll get back together.

**Major Dramatic Question of *Late For Dinner*:**
**Will the Guy Be Able to Reclaim His Woman**
**After He's Been Frozen for 29 Years?**
**Answer:**
*Yes*.

He came back and reclaimed her. But then he had to live with her and deal with her as a grown woman with all her complexities and experiences and baggage.

Because Act III never dealt with this, the audience was lost and the movie tanked.

## Why a Weak Third Act
## Is Like Bad Sex

Writing a screenplay is not only telling a story, it's selling a story.

There's an old salesman's maxim: *Always be closing*. Roughly translated, it means a good salesman must relentlessly push his client to buy. As a screenwriter, you must relentlessly push your audience to "buy" what you're giving them on the pages of your script.

You start the sale by luring your audience in and hooking them immediately with the expectation of a nifty tale to come (Act I). Then you let them settle in and take a slow, but ever-intensifying uphill ride in a roller coaster that rests for a brief moment on the top of the tracks, where there's no turning back, and nowhere to go but *full steam ahead* into the final stages of the tale in which you've ensnared them (Act III).

Now comes closing the sale.

Think of your Act III as the symbolic ride down the roller coaster. Like the real thing, the ride down has to be faster and more exhilarating than the ride up. The ride up is all about expectation, possibilities, and anticipation.

The ride down is about getting questions answered, new questions posed, finding relief from the tension you've felt, and, ultimately, satisfaction.

A *strong* close by a good salesman results in the sale. He's happy. The client's happy. They're each getting something out of the time they've spent together.

A *weak* close means the salesman's lost the sale. Maybe he lost his concentration, took the client for granted, lost his confidence, showed his desperation, or just ran out of steam. Whatever, the sale is gone. But a strong third act is like the good close. You and your audience are happy and you've both gotten something out of the time you spent together.

Which is why a weak third act is like bad sex: it happens too fast, takes too long, or doesn't even get you turned on.

# Strategy

## Act II-and-a-Half

Think of this as the second exclamation point. An event occurring in approximately the last five minutes of a script that sends the story into yet another new and enthralling unforeseen direction. A variation on this with regard to character arc comes from the renowned Russian acting teacher, Stanislavski, who said that the last ninety seconds of a play are the most important for the protagonist because it is during this time that the main character experiences an irreversible moment of truth.

He realizes there's no turning back. The die is cast. Simultaneously, the protagonist experiences a new sense of awareness. To observe great examples of this powerful effect, check out the following films and examine the last five minutes: *Schindler's List*, *It's a Wonderful Life*, *On the Waterfront*, *Seven Beauties*, *The Sixth Sense*, and *Rain Man*.

## Writing Exercise

Complex, three-dimensional characters are the most interesting. This means giving your protagonist an inner conflict, as well as an external conflict. Inner conflicts can be as simple as a smart woman who is insecure about her intelligence or a particular talent she has.

Does the protagonist of your current or previous screenplay have an inner conflict? Is it "big" enough? Make a list of potential inner conflicts for the two lead roles in your script.

CHAPTER 15

# The Irony of Irony

*"Love is an ideal thing, marriage a real thing. Confusion of the real with the ideal never goes unpunished."*
— Johann Wolfgang von Goethe

How often does something dramatic (good or bad, big or small) happen to you? Something interesting enough to merit telling someone about it?

For most of us, nothing out of the ordinary happens all that often. For a few, something cathartic occurs. And often, within that dramatic event we experience, there is dramatic irony permeating it.

A friend recounted how he had gone to a nightclub on the Lower East Side. While he was there, someone had been killed in a knife fight. In recounting the story, the dramatic experience was that he was there and saw the person die. Frightening and interesting, but not ironic. At least not for him.

A few days later I happened to be talking to my mother in Ohio. She casually mentioned that a guy who lived two blocks away from her had been murdered in New York the previous weekend. Other than the strangeness in hearing that someone from my old neighborhood — a person who had resided two blocks from the house I'd grown up in — had been murdered in New York, I didn't pay much more attention. But then when my mother read me the news story in her local paper, it dawned on me that the murder victim was the person my friend had seen die.

That's irony.

So much of life is filled with it. And so much of the irony of life is dramatic.

When I think of the irony I've experienced, observed, or shared with friends, it comes off like all the Shakespearean and Greek tragedies combined with the grit of a hardboiled Raymond Chandler novel, mixed in with the neurotic hysteria of a Tennessee Williams play.

In other words, it's been, well, ironic.

The following are examples of irony. They're all true. Some are serious, others amusing.

- The father of a friend of mine was a leader in his church and a devout Catholic, considered by many to be the most religious man in town. He also had sex with his own daughters, even making one pregnant.

- The high school girlfriend of a friend was the quintessential dim-witted, giddy, cloyingly childlike, self-involved beauty. It was understood that she had never read a book in high school and hadn't read one in her adult life either. It was also understood that she didn't read the newspaper or pay attention to current events. Nevertheless, she went on to become a successful real estate agent making a huge salary. She's middle-aged now, still gorgeous, dimwitted, and *wealthy.*

- A gay friend of mine loved to shock me with tales of his wild sexual behavior (prior to AIDS). He was into multiple partners, orgies, S&M, and a whole catalog of other sexual debaucheries. But the time he shocked me most was his story of the man he picked and *didn't* have sex with. All they did was kiss passionately for two hours. Just kissing. Some nuzzling on the neck. Some tonguing in the ear. Nothing else. He was thirty-five years old and been actively sexually since he was fifteen, but had never, literally, been kissed.

▓ I live in New York City, a place with perhaps a more visible homeless population than most towns. Recently I moved. Moves in Manhattan often entail relocating only a few blocks away, but in a city as concentrated as New York, those few blocks might as well be twenty-five miles. I found different places to take dry cleaning, buy food, get a newspaper, a new route to a movie theater. In my new neighborhood there were also homeless people. In Manhattan, you see them and co-exist. But one day, a few months after my move, I encountered one of the homeless men from my old neighborhood. He was going through a garbage can. I was walking my dog. Actually, I spotted him at the exact time he saw me. There was a definite sense of recognition. I know he thought what I thought: *You're in a new neighborhood.* For a split second I almost said hello, but as I had never spoken to him in my old neighborhood, I decided against it now. Besides, what was there to say? The irony of this haunted me for weeks.

# Writing Exercise

Make a list of the five most ironic things you've experienced directly or indirectly. You'll find that each one makes you sit back and think. And ponder. And maybe shake your head over how truly peculiar and sadly amusing life can be. All of which can be used in your screenplays.

# Strategy

## The Value of Old Movies

Old movies from the 1930s and 1940s are great lessons in screenwriting. They're strong on plot, they get started fast, there's very little exposition or backstory, and *Citizen Kane* and *Gone with the Wind* notwithstanding, they were shorter back then.

Watch vintage films on American Movie Classics, Turner Classic Movies, or Netflix and notice their running times, both classics and "B" movies. Most are less than one-hundred minutes. Some are less than ninety minutes or barely crack eighty.

You'll also learn something about dialogue. In the early days of Hollywood, screenwriters were up against censorship through the strict and upright Hayes Office, so they had to be less obvious and more clever. There's a lesson in this. It's easy to write X-rated, edgy dialogue. It's hard to keep it clean but still be clever and hip. Here are some of my favorites: *Scarlet Street*, *Double Indemnity*, *The Lady Eve*, *Of Mice and Men*, and *Black Narcissus*.

CHAPTER 16

# The Single Bullet Theory of the JFK Assassination and How It Can Help the Plotting of Your Screenplay

*"Lee Harvey Oswald acted alone."*

— Conclusion of the Warren Report

I've always been intrigued by the many theories surrounding the assassination of President John. F. Kennedy on November 22, 1963. I have never been convinced that Lee Harvey Oswald alone shot the president, and I firmly believe there was a second gunman.

But it wasn't until I saw Oliver Stone's *JFK* and watched the courtroom scene, where Kevin Costner diagrams the convoluted path that purports to explain the single bullet theory, that it dawned on me that good writing follows a similar path.

If you never saw the film or if you aren't familiar with the single bullet theory, it goes something like this:

There are those who are convinced that one bullet was responsible for the death of President Kennedy and the wounds received by Texas Governor John Connelly. According to their single bullet theory, the same bullet that was fired into the back of JFK's head tumbled downward and to the right, managed to go through the President's own chest, through Governor Connelly's right shoulder and into his right wrist.

Whether true or not, the underlying aspect of the theory is fascinating from a storytelling point of view.

The trajectory of a bullet is predictable until the instant it strikes something... anything. After that instant, it can go in any direction and come to rest anywhere. The best screenplays (and all stories for that matter) are like that: In a single moment, their plots are transformed with unexpected twists, unforeseen revelations, ingenious wrinkles, and unanticipated reversals.

It's intriguing to think a storyline is going in one direction only to find out it's going in another and that *that* direction is one that never crossed your mind as a possibility. And when the screenwriter is really clever he tops *that* surprise with another. And another after that.

Make a list of five movies you've seen that genuinely surprised you with amazing plot turns, twists, and reversals. Then rent them. Then study them in the privacy of your own home.

Since you've already seen the films, you aren't watching them for enjoyment. This is work. An assignment. Study hall.

And even though this homework is watching a movie, it shouldn't be taken lightly. Don't watch it with anyone else. Sit in front of the screen by yourself with a pen and notebook.

Here's what to look for:

- The points in the film when you thought one thing was going to happen, but something else occurred.

- The points in the film when something happened that came totally out of left field, but was ultimately logical.

- The event in the last 10 minutes of the film that you never-in-a-million-years thought was coming.

- The event in the last 60 seconds of the film that you never expected.

The following are five films that were filled with one after another unexpected turns of plot.

*The Deer Hunter, Tell No One, The Vanishing* (1988), *Waking Ned Devine,* and *Wanted* (2008).

Enjoy. Then study!

# Strategy

## The Fifty-First Girl

The most frequently used word in Hollywood is *no.* It's short, easy to understand, and speaks volumes. It's safer to say than *yes* and easier to live with than *yes,* because *yes* is a commitment. Contracts have to be drawn up. Checks have to be written. Dozens of phone calls have to be made. Asses must be put on the line. Who wants to risk their ass and potentially their career when a simple *no* will enable you to live and fight and, well, say *no* another day You will hear the two-letter word more often than any other.

Every screenwriter hears it, even the established, up-per-echelon people. It's part of the package. You'll never like hearing it, but for your own peace of mind, get used to it.

Just take it in and move on. Getting a *no* response to your screenplay reminds me of the guy who asks out a girl. She says *no*. He finds another girl. Asks her. Again, *no*. He keeps asking and keeps getting told *no*. He hits number fifty. *No*. But then comes the fifty-first girl. She says, "Yes. I'd love to go out with you." Before the words are out of her mouth, he's forgotten every previous *no* and he's concentrating on the *yes*. This is how it is when you hear the three-letter word about your screenplay. All the two-letter words will evaporate into a quickly forgotten mist.

# Writing Exercise

Challenge yourself:

If you're a comedy writer, write something serious and dark.

If you write drama, write something comedic.

If you write action/adventure, write a gentle coming-of-age story.

If your style is Indie, write a mainstream Hollywood studio picture.

The reason to do this is to find out if you harbor an undiscovered ability to write something outside of your comfort zone.

CHAPTER 17

# Having Trouble Finding Story Ideas? Look Backward.

*"No one returns with goodwill to the place which has done him mischief."*

— Phaedrus

I'm one of those people blessed (or cursed, depending upon your point of view) with a flypaper-like mind that is a repository for tons of useless, meaningless details from my past.

Stuff like how I felt in first grade when I announced to the class that my sister was born and no one cared. I remember crying and feeling bad because the only reason I brought it up was because another boy (I even remember his name) was singled out by the teacher (I don't remember her name) because *his* sister had just been born. Logic dictated to my 6-year-old mind that if he was being singled out for having a new sister, so should I. Wrong.

Now, I've got lots and lots of memories like this. Things that I wish I could forget. And from what most people tell me when I tell them about this memory of mine, they aren't like me. They've forgotten crap like this. The only good thing about this "ability" is that it opens up all kinds of windows to remember events from my youth that I can use.

Here's a story from when I was in high school. A friend of mine fixed me up on a blind date. The girl's and my only communication had been one telephone conversation during which I asked her to go to a dance at my high school — an all-boys Catholic school. The conversation was uneventful except for one piece of information she revealed.

She hated guys who wore glasses.

Ouch! I wore glasses. No problem, I figured. I'll just take them off before I pick her up, then put them on when I drive, pointing out that I need them for driving. It made sense to me. It really did. And it worked, too. Until we got to the dance.

What I hadn't counted on was the fact that everyone who knew me knew that I wore glasses. So when you're used to seeing someone with glasses who's not wearing them, you might tend to remark, "Where's your glasses?"

Which is what happened. After the sixth guy had re-marked about the absence of my glasses, I could tell by the sneer on my date's face that she loathed me. We ended up leaving early and I took her home and that was that. Pathetic, right? I was brimming with self-esteem, right? But it's fun to tell now. Actually, it was kind of fun to tell a couple of days after it happened. But when I was living through it, I wanted to die of embarrassment.

Although back then I didn't know what a "character arc" was, I experienced one that taught me a lesson: Never lie about yourself to a woman.

Here's another winner from my youth.

Seventh grade. I had a crush on a girl and at recess one day I made the mistake of telling a guy in the class my secret. He promised he wouldn't tell the girl, whom he happened to sit next to in class. Fifteen minutes later, as the class was filtering back into the classroom, I happened to turn around and overhear the kid say to the girl, "Guess who likes you?" Then he told her, to which she replied with a grotesque grimace, "Eewwwwwoooo."

I was devastated. And I immediately stopped liking her.

Jump ahead five years. I'm a senior in high school. I'm walking down a neighborhood street and I see a car pull up. Two guys and a girl are in the car. The car stops and the passenger side of the door flies open.

I hear a guy yell, "Get the hell out, you whore." And who do I see scrambling out of the car but the girl in my seventh-grade class who was so unimpressed that I liked her.

Our eyes met. We hadn't seen each other since eighth grade. She recognized me. I remember the moment as if it were yesterday. We didn't acknowledge each other. She was still clearly upset and embarrassed at being called a whore by the guys who kicked her out of the car.

I kept walking. I was also secretly glad. But I also felt a slight tinge of compassion for her. Very slight.

The point of these two anecdotes is that they're both small events in my life that were powerful enough to affect me. They were little movies with beginnings, middles, and endings. And over the years I've related them in classrooms or to friends sharing their adolescent war stories.

# Writing Exercise

I know you have a few memories like mine. Some might be as fresh in your memory as if they happened yesterday. Others may be only a thin haze in your mind. Think hard. Remember the pain or embarrassment. Write down every detail. You might laugh about it now and there might be a movie in it.

# Strategy

### Somebody Has to Say You're Good

No one succeeds on his or her own. Sure, some get a head start because they're born wealthy or into a family with connections. There's an understanding that, once they're ready to begin a career, phone calls will be made and jobs will be gotten whether they're qualified or not. Others make their own connections; the internship or part-time job that leads to something. School ties help some get their foot in the door. Dating the right person is another way in.

Then there are the rest of us who don't know a soul, go to the wrong schools, and join the wrong clubs (if we join anything at all). We're lousy at networking and schmoozing because we're shy, unassertive, or socially inept. We have greater odds against succeeding and consequently, from a dramatic point of view, are more interesting to watch.

Same with a movie. The wealthy or connected person with the same problem as the unconnected regular guy will handle it differently. He can call his dad or frat brother or whomever. The regular Joe can't call anybody. He's on his own as he tries to resolve his crisis. Now, in the real world he'll most likely get totally screwed and wind up crashing and burning — unless he gets someone to help him. In writing a screenplay, your help comes from allies and mentors. These are the individuals who pop in and out of your life offering advice, consolation, and wisdom. The value of allies and mentors in your storytelling is incalculable.

CHAPTER 18

# And Then What?

*"By a small sample we may judge of the whole piece."*

— Miguel de Cervantes

An idea that isn't complete stinks like a dead fish. Unfortunately, everybody knows it but you.

It's like the wife of the philandering husband being the last to find out her mate is schtupping his secretary, the church organist, and half of her bowling team.

I've heard enough students pitch ideas for scripts they want to write and I've pitched enough of my own to hear the three most dreaded words:

"And then what?"

"And then what?" is the response of someone (producer, development person, friend, parent, child) who has listened to you talk out your new storyline. And the look on her face is a blank, sympathetic, or confused stare that says you haven't piqued her interest, or worse, that you've lost her, or even worse, that you've bored her.

The problem with having "And then what?" asked of you is that it makes you look bad. Amateurish. Like you haven't done your homework or weren't professional enough to have spent enough time getting your story down.

How do you avoid hearing these words? Make sure you've thought your story through. Know where all the pivotal plot points come. Know where the act-breaks fall. Know what your main character wants. Have a clear idea of how the story will end.

And then what?

Practice talking out your story to yourself. Out loud. Sit in front of a mirror and talk. Get used to hearing your own voice.

And then what?

You'll be ready to do it for real.

And then what?

You'll sound like someone who has prepared.

And then what?

Maybe, just maybe, the person you tell it to will say the sweetest words a screenwriter can hear: "I like it."

# Strategy

### When You and Your Screenplay
### Have Irreconcilable Differences

I think the biggest problem all screenwriters face is that we get lost in our own point of view. In the early stages of the screenwriting process, getting lost in our scripts is good. It's what launches us. But that kind of single-mindedness can only take us so far. At some point we have to pull back and be more objective and self-critical.

The further we allow ourselves to go into our own little wormhole, the easier it is to become imprisoned there. Once that happens, it's easy to be overwhelmed by and deluded by our personal visions.

It's a matter of getting back your focus. It's like falling back in love with your material. Think of you and your script as having had a huge lover's quarrel. You're not speaking. You've separated, maybe even divorced. You might even have started working on another script which is tantamount to cheating. But you want to come back and your screenplay is ready to welcome you so the two of you can try again.

A good way to accomplish this reconciliation is by doing things you've heard before. Maybe you've tried them. Maybe not. Maybe it's time.

## 10 Best Ways to Reconnect to Your Screenplay

1. Retype your entire screenplay from page one. It'll help you get back into the feel of where you left off.

2. Set a writing schedule you won't veer from.

3. Give yourself a daily page goal — even if it's only one page.

4. Edit any scene that seems too talkie or has too many stage directions.

5. Take a scalpel to all overwritten stage directions. For most scenes, less is more.

6. If a scene is tormenting you, maybe it shouldn't be there. Every scene must have a dramatic purpose. If it doesn't, cut it.

7. Try to write *something* every day. Even if it's only a long email to someone.

8. Give yourself an imaginary deadline to complete your script.

9. Go over the preliminary notes you made when you first had the idea for the screenplay. You might find a thought or idea you've forgotten that gets you re-focused.

10. Watch movies. Sometimes losing yourself in a film, good or bad, will get your juices flowing again.

Without sounding too new age, the object is to get into a mindset that will guide you into that wonderful zone where you're totally into the material.

You're in love again!

# Writing Exercise

Write three love scenes.

1) An inept, pathologically shy guy tries to ask out a girl he's had a crush on for years.

2) An older guy who thinks of himself as a player asks out a younger woman who thinks he's too old for her.

3) A confident, overly aggressive woman used to getting her way falls hard for an equally confident man and she decides to ask him out, but he is clearly disinterested.

CHAPTER 19

# The Necessity of Treatments

*"An original story written for motion picture purposes in a form suitable for use as the basis of a screenplay."*

— Definition of a Treatment

For some screenwriters, treatments are a waste of time. Considering the energy you put into writing one, you might as well just write the screenplay.

I'm an outline guy. Get the basic three-act structure down and start the freakin' script. Unfortunately, the day will come when you may *have* to write one so it's good to know how to do it. You've written a screenplay that gets you an agent or some attention from a producer. They like your script, but they don't want to make it. But they want to work with you.

Maybe they have the kernel of an idea for a movie, or they've asked you to pitch more ideas of yours, or they want to hire you to adapt a book or play.

Bottom line, they hire you for a project. Odds are, they'll want you to do a treatment before you start the script. Many writers have "pitch" meetings where they talk out concepts and ideas. Some writers get deals on the pitch alone. But before they start the screenplay, many will have to turn in a treatment first.

That's why it's important to learn how to write one.

The nature of a treatment is such that it lays out the entire storyline in narrative form. There is some dialogue, but not that much, just snippets here and there to get across the point of a scene. If I were to set out to write the screenplay, I would have a tightly detailed blueprint to follow.

This is not to say that I wouldn't veer from that blueprint. But I might. A scene may not work. An idea for a scene or plot twist that I hadn't thought of might pop into my head and take me in another direction.

Most importantly, the treatment is ready to be turned into a screenplay. Key characters are here, the motivation of the major characters is established, the act breaks come at the right places, and I know how it's going to end.

Use this as a guide for any length treatment you will write.

What follows are the three-act outline and treatment I wrote for a screenplay called *Dashing Through the Snow*. Because the structure was so clear in my head the outline is shorter than usual.

### Act I

Seven-year-old kid wants to sue Santa Claus for malpractice. He gets the idea after helping his mother study for a law exam. She's going to law school at night. He goes to the phone book and starts cold-calling lawyers. He finds one named Nolan who will take the case.

His mother finds out what he's doing and goes to meet the lawyer with him because she's suspicious as to the guy's motives.

At the meeting the lawyer explains why he's taking the case. He has personal reasons going back to his family history. He claims that he's descended from elves.

### Act II

The kid's mom naturally thinks the lawyer is nuts and drags her son out of his office. The lawyer persists and gradually gains the trust of mom. A romantic subplot begins.

Complicating things is the fact that someone is following the lawyer. We learn that lawyers from Santa Claus have heard about the impending lawsuit.

We learn that the lawyer and his father (also a lawyer) don't get along. The father doesn't hold the grudge against Santa Claus that his son does.

The lawyer, the 7-year-old, and his mom join forces to build their case against Santa Claus. They need witnesses so they go about trying to find them.

Build to end-of-Act-II revelation that Nolan was wrong about being descended from elves. He's really descended from Santa Claus!

## Act III

Ultimate confrontation between the lawyer and Santa Claus, who is in poor health and must retire. A replacement is needed. Surprise ending is that the lawyer's father will take over as the new Santa Claus.

The lawyer marries the 7-year-old's mom, officially adopts the kid, and we end with the realization that the kid will someday be the next Santa Claus.

# TREATMENT
## *Dashing Through the Snow*
### Written by
### D. B. Gilles

## PREMISE

A seven-year-old boy hires a lawyer to sue Santa Claus for malpractice and both discover more than they bargained for.

### ACT I
### SUPER — Two Weeks Before Christmas

The face of Santa Claus fills the screen. Specifically, the classic drawing by Thomas Nast of Santa with a flowing white beard, blustery red cheeks, bright eyes, and a glowing smile.

Suddenly — something flies into frame and nails Santa on the nose. It's chocolate pudding. It oozes over his lips and beard.

PULLBACK REVEALS that we're in an elementary school hallway and a feisty, smirking seven-year-old boy is the guilty culprit.

Meet SCOTT WOODBURY. Think Jack Black in second grade. He looks pleased with his work. He's about to throw something else when a hand grabs his right arm. It's a teacher catching him in the act.

Principal's office. Scott's being reprimanded, but he sits there unintimidated. Why did he throw pudding at Santa Claus? "Because I hate Santa Claus." He goes into a Dennis Miller–like rant on how rotten Santa is. The principal refers to an open file on her desk — Scott's file — and remarks that every Christmas for the last two years he has become disruptive. "You give me no choice other than to call your mother."

Corporate office. HOLLY WOODBURY, 28, Scott's mom, is at her desk. She's a full-time paralegal. What she lacks in self-confidence she makes up for with sincerity. She goes to law school part-time at night. Her phone rings. It's the principal. All Holly says is, "Not again."

Holly sits across from the principal. In her hands is a drawing by Scott. The letters spelling SANTA CLAUS have been altered to read SATAN CLAWS. We see Scott through a glass divider sitting in the outer office. Holly says, "My husband and I divorced three years ago. Scott took it hard. Especially around Christmas. That's when his father left."

Holly and Scott leaving the school. She's laying into him. "You're behaving like a little Scrooge again. Refusing to sing Christmas carols, defiling the picture of Santa Claus, telling everyone that Santa sucks." Scott says nothing.

Their one-bedroom apartment. Nothing fancy. A Christmas tree stands in the corner. Scott helps Holly do the dinner dishes. She's telling him how glad she is that her fall semester is ending. We learn that her company is paying her law school tuition, but she's insecure whether or not she has what it takes to be a lawyer. Scott builds up her confidence, telling her that she'll be the best lawyer ever. She asks Scott to help her study for an exam. She talks to him like he's a little adult.

Later. Scott helps Holly study legal terms. He asks her the difference between malpractice and negligence. She explains; malpractice is more like incompetence. He asks her what incompetence means. She says, "Not doing something very well."

Scott says that when she becomes a lawyer he's going to hire her to sue Santa Claus for malpractice. Holly says, "Sweetie, you can't sue Santa Claus."

Scott gives her a "why not" look. She's about to say, "Because he doesn't exist," but catches herself. "I thought you didn't believe in Santa." Scott admits that he really does.

To placate him she says, "Tell you what, when I become a lawyer you'll be my first client." This pleases Scott.

Holly's office. She's telling her co-worker, SYLVIA, that she didn't have the heart to tell Scott that you can't sue somebody who doesn't exist. Sylvia tells her about the new man she met. He has a friend. Holly tells her she's too overwhelmed to date what with working, going to law school, and taking care of Scott. She also adds that "It's gonna take me a long time to believe in love again."

Scott at school. The teacher is using the children's classic *The Little Engine That Could* to illustrate the point that if we set our minds to do something, we can. All it takes is perseverance. This gets Scott to thinking.

Scott and Holly's apartment. Scott's babysitter, an elderly Italian woman, sits on the couch reading. Scott's watching TV. A commercial comes on for one of those sleazy law firms. Scott hears the announcer say, "You pay nothing unless we win. All cases are on a contingency basis."

Scott mouths the word *contingency*. CUT TO: Scott looking up the word *contingency* in one of Holly's law textbooks.

CUT TO: Scott looking at the LAWYERS section in the Manhattan Yellow Pages. Sees thousands of names. He's bummed. He goes to the family computer and performs a search for "lawyers in New York City". He lands on a link that says there are over 20,000 lawyers in Manhattan.

He thinks, types in the words *malpractice lawyers* and hits ENTER. This narrows the search somewhat, but the figure is still huge. He thinks, then types in his ZIP code. This reduces the figure to 241. He hits PRINT.

Later. Scott has the printout of 241 malpractice lawyers in front of him. He starts calling, saying he wants to sue Santa Claus for malpractice and he needs a lawyer to take the case on a contingency basis. Dissolving shots show him leaving messages, being brushed off by secretaries or by the lawyers themselves.

He comes to the letter E: Ellway & Ellway. We hear their voice mail. "To leave a message for Nolan Ellway Jr., press one. For Nolan Ellway Sr., press two." Scott presses one. Starts his spiel.

CUT TO: NOLAN ELLWAY JR., 28, at his desk. Hyper, but sweet. A framed law degree from NYU hangs on the wall. He tries to open a container of coffee. He spills it on the papers on his desk. As he cleans up the mess he listens to his messages.

Scott's message plays. Nolan listens to it with great interest. He smiles excitedly. Writes down Scott's number.

Later. Holly is soaking in the bathtub. Scott's in the living room watching TV. Phone rings. Holly calls out that she's too tired to talk to anyone. "Let the answering machine pick up." Scott says OK. He listens to the message and hears:

"This is for Scott Woodbury. My name is Nolan Ellway Junior. You left a message about wanting to sue Santa Claus for malpractice. I'm interested in taking the case. Call me at your earliest convenience." He leaves his phone number.

Stunned, Scott replays the message. Writes down the phone number. Dials it.

Nolan's office. Phone rings. It's Scott. Nolan perks up. Says he wants to meet the next day. Scott says he has to ask his mother. "Your *what?*" Nolan is puzzled.

"Ask me what?" says Holly. She stands behind Scott in her robe, fresh out of the tub. Scott hangs up. Holly asks whom he was talking to. Scott hems and haws. Holly looks at the answering machine. Plays the message. Scott tells her how he called a bunch of lawyers.

Holly hits redial. Nolan answers. She identifies herself and asks if he knows that Scott Woodbury is a seven-year-old boy. He didn't. Nolan remarks that the voice did sound awfully high-pitched. She tells him that if he's calling because he thinks he can make some quick money by taking a case that a judge will throw out of court, he's made a mistake. She emphasizes that she's in law school and that she knows how the law works.

Nolan says he's not interested in money, that he'll do it entirely pro bono and that he can promise her it won't be a frivolous lawsuit. She's about to hang up when he says that there's a precedent for this case. She says, "Are you saying somebody tried to sue Santa Claus for malpractice before?"

He says not for malpractice. Something else. Still skeptical, she demands to know what. "I'd rather not discuss it on the phone. Can we meet?" He promises her a wealth of evidence. She agrees to meet him the next day on her lunch hour.

Next day. Holly arrives at the offices of Ellway & Ellway. The receptionist sends her into Nolan's office. Holly has a "this better be good" attitude.

Nolan fills her in on the details of the precedent-setting lawsuit against Santa Claus. Specifically, it was a lawsuit filed in 1892 by a man claiming to be an elf who worked for Santa Claus. "An *elf?*" says Holly.

Nolan continues. "In 1892 the elf was denied employment by Santa Claus because he was six foot eight inches and was banished from the North Pole. He came to the United States, settled in Maine, hired a lawyer and sued Santa Claus for job discrimination. Ultimately the case was thrown out of court."

Holly has a major problem with the elf issue. Nolan says, "In anticipation of your reaction, I went online directly to the judge's written opinion. I printed out this hard copy for you to read." He hands it to her.

Sure enough. It reads "Elfman v Claus."

Holly smirks. "First you want me to believe that Santa Claus is real. Now you're trying to convince me that elves exist too."

"They do," he says. "I can prove it."

She says, "How?"

He says, "You're looking at one."

**?**

## ACT II

"You're telling me that you're... an elf?"

"I'm *descended* from elves. I don't actually think of myself as an elf."

"You're nuts!" She storms out of his office. Nolan follows her. Holly makes a sarcastic remark about elves. NOLAN ELLWAY SR, a small, gruff-looking man in his fifties, overhears what Holly said. He looks concerned. Nolan Jr. follows Holly into the hallway to the elevator. He's begging her to believe him. "Elves are real. Just like Santa Claus is real."

She says, "Everybody knows Santa Claus was made up. Everybody knows that *parents* put presents under Christmas trees. Santa Claus *doesn't* come down the chimney."

Elevator comes. He follows her inside.

Nolan deals with her skepticism by asking her if she believes in UFOs. She says no. "Some people do," he says. "Some people believe in aliens, Bigfoot, and the Loch Ness monster. But nobody believes in Santa Claus except little kids. And they believe until some other kid tells them that there's no such thing. By then they leave part of their childhood behind and they buy into the concept that there's no such thing as Santa Claus."

Elevator doors open. Nolan follows her out onto the street. "And by the time kids grow up they've long forgotten about Santa Claus and whether he exists until they have their own kids and perpetuate the lie."

She says, "How can Santa Claus be real? I mean, the flying sleigh? The reindeer? Going down the chimney?"

Nolan says, "A lot of that is myth, skillfully sustained by Santa's publicists, not to mention brilliant spin control."

Holly replies, "If Santa Claus exists, why hasn't he been exposed? I mean, this case is from 1892. Hasn't some lawyer stumbled onto this case before? Even accidentally?"

Nolan explains. "First of all, the statute of limitations ran out after fifty years. Back in 1892 fewer people were educated or sophisticated. And the concept of Santa Claus wasn't like it is today with commercialism and whatnot. The case was in a remote corner of the Northeast. Nobody knew about it. Nobody cared about it."

"Why do you?" she asks.

"I told you."

She gives him a look. "Oh. *Right.* You're an *elf!* Listen, you freak. Stay away from me and my son." She walks away.

Frustrated, Nolan heads back to his office building. CAM TILTS UP to see Nolan Sr. watching him.

When Nolan gets to his office, his father is there to meet him. "What was that all about?" Nolan says nothing. His father pushes. "You got somebody who wants to sue him, right?" Nolan says no. His father warns him: "Let it go. Don't mess with the man in red."

Fordham law library. Holly sits at a table. Before her, along with the Internet printout of the 1892 lawsuit, is the law book that contains the case. She's reading the judge's opinion.

Holly's in the office of one of her law professors. He's reading the 1892 case law. From the gist of their conversation he's confirming that somebody claiming to be an elf did indeed sue Santa Claus for job discrimination. But it doesn't necessarily mean Santa Claus is real.

Because Holly doesn't believe that Nolan is an elf, she doesn't bring it up. But she does tell the professor how Nolan believes the 1892 case proves Santa Claus exists and that he wants to sue him again by representing her son.

"The law is on the lawyer's side," says the professor. "If he makes a good case he definitely has a shot at going to trial." Holly says, "The entire thesis of the case is that Santa Claus is real, but everyone knows he isn't."

The professor says, "Common sense says Santa doesn't exist. But if this lawyer can prove he does, it'll be the trial of the century."

CUT TO: Nolan in a bar. The bartender is putting Christmas decorations up and remarking that he's never sure how long he should wait to take down the decorations. Another customer offers an explanation. Nolan corrects the guy, then starts talking about various historical facts about Christmas. The bartender comments on how much Nolan knows. "You'd be surprised how much I know."

A Blockbuster store. Holly and Scott are looking for movies to rent. Holly notices a special stack of Christmas-oriented movies. One grabs her attention: a documentary called — *Santa Claus and His Elves: Fact or Fiction?* Holly picks it up.

CUT TO: Holly inserting the DVD into their player. She joins Scott on the couch, fast-forwards through the Santa Claus material, and goes straight to the part about the elves.

She learns much information, mainly that elves have supposedly been in the world as long as man, that elves settled at the North Pole and worked for Santa Claus. Elves are smaller in size than Santa Claus, but their age is not known to anyone, not even to themselves.

When it's over, Holly sits and thinks. She doesn't know what to make of it. She goes to the phone. Dials Nolan's number.

Nolan's apartment. Phone rings. It's Holly. She says, "Say I believe that you're descended from an elf and that Santa Claus is real. Why do *you* want to sue Santa Claus? My kid is seven. He at least has a reason."

"I'd rather tell you in person. Let's meet for coffee." She says she can't leave Scott alone. He says bring him along. Manhattan street. Holly and Scott walking. She tells him that the lawyer might be saying unbelievable things. "Like what?" "That his great-great-grandfather was an elf who used to work for Santa Claus." Scott gives her a look. She says, "Just listen. If we agree he's crazy, we'll leave." Scott nods okay.

Starbucks. Nolan is waiting. Holly introduces Scott and Nolan. Nolan says, "So you want to sue Santa Claus for malpractice, eh?" Scott nods yes. Nolan says, "We can also get him for negligence, fraud, racketeering, and a dozen other crimes. We can even get him for driving a sleigh without a license." Scott smiles, says, "Dude!" Nolan smiles back. They high-five.

Holly asks Nolan what his motive is for suing Santa Claus. He explains that his great-great-grandfather was a broken man upon being banished from the North Pole. He was Santa's right-hand elf. Close not only to Santa, but Mrs. Claus and their kids.

"*Mrs.* Claus?" says Scott.

"My great-great-grandfather started a new life in America. He kept it secret that he was an elf. He never said a word until he was on his deathbed. Then he revealed the truth before he passed away. Our real name is Elfman, not Ellway." Scott and Holly look at each other, not sure what to believe.

Nolan continues. "That's what started our family obsession with suing Santa Claus. My grandfather became a lawyer for the sole purpose of getting even. But he realized early on how resourceful Santa Claus was. Santa Claus has a powerful law firm. Their only client is Santa Claus. Their name is Donner, Dancer, Blitzer & Epstein. They broke my grandfather's spirit."

Holly and Scott are riveted. From the look on her face, she's starting to believe what she's hearing.

"Grampa spent all his energy pursuing legal avenues to re-open the 1892 case. Nobody took him seriously. It was the thirties and forties. The Depression was on. World War Two. People needed Christmas. Santa Claus was loved by everyone. My grandfather gave up because he knew he couldn't win. My father's a lawyer too. He just wants to put it all behind him. I got involved because I was so close to my grandfather. I've been waiting my whole life to avenge the dismissal of my grandfather's own grandfather."

He looks at Scott. "When I got your call I knew my chance had come." Holly says, "I understand *why* you want to do this, but I don't know what you want to accomplish from doing it."

Nolan says, "The world will be a better place without the commercialism of Christmas. Who better represents that than Santa Claus? No more little kids being disappointed. No more families going into debt buying junk."

Holly takes it in. "I hardly ever got what I wanted for Christmas." But she *still* resists believing that Santa Claus is real. She says she needs to think about it. Scott protests. He's ready to rumble. But Holly says not yet.

As they leave, a goofy-looking guy wearing a red beret in the next booth pulls out his cell and dials a number. "He's got a live one." CUT TO: Nolan Sr. in his office. He tells Red Beret to stay on top of it.

Red Beret leaves Starbucks. He walks at a fast clip, then suddenly he's flanked on each side by two short, chubby men, each barely over five feet tall. They pull him into an alley and demand to know what he overheard in the booth. He tells them. They leave him alone, shaking.

He immediately phones Nolan Sr. and tells him what happened. Nolan Sr. replies, "Don't worry about it. All it means is that the man-in-red's people are trying to scare us."

The law firm of Donner, Dancer, Blitzer & Epstein. The two short, chubby guys are in the office of ELLIOT BLITZER: a slick, cool, mean man. He instructs the chubby guys to find out everything about Holly and to bug Nolan's phones and home.

Nolan walks Holly and Scott home. He asks her to make a decision soon. She says she will. Later, in their apartment, Scott says how much he likes Nolan and, more importantly, that he believes him. He begs Holly to authorize going forward with the lawsuit. She still wants to think about it.

Nolan's office. Night. One of the chubby guys, dressed as a janitor, dismantles the telephone and installs a miniature recording device. CUT TO: The other chubby guy bugging Nolan's apartment.

Holly at work. She gets another call from the principal of Scott's school. "What?" Holly meets with the principal. This time she tells her Scott's done a complete turnaround, telling everybody that Santa Claus is real and that he's going to sue him and that he's hired a lawyer who's an elf and on and on. Holly smoothes things over by saying that Scott has a vivid imagination and that she'll get him counseling.

Holly reprimands Scott for having a big mouth. She says if he says another word to anyone, she won't allow Nolan to be his lawyer. This straightens out Scott.

Next morning. Holly's getting Scott ready for school. Phone rings. A mysterious voice says that if she refuses to allow Nolan Ellway to take her son's case, she'll be given $100,000. She demands to know who it is. The voice continues. "You can do a lot with $100,000. Think about it."

Holly calls Nolan. Tells him. He says, "They've gotten to you." "*Who's* gotten to me?" "His people." "*Whose* people?" "Santa Claus." Nolan says they shouldn't talk on the phone. Suggests they meet in a public place because she'll probably be followed. They agree to meet at the law library at Fordham.

Later. Holly walks Scott to school. She tells him not to tell anyone about Nolan or the lawsuit. She walks off to catch a bus. Someone is watching her. PULLBACK REVEALS that it's the two chubby guys.

Holly at work, meeting with her boss. She has to drop off some legal papers to a client. She leaves her office building. The chubby guys follower her. Following *them* is Red Beret. She enters another building. Gets in an elevator. The chubby guys get in and stop the elevator. One hands her something.

INSERT: a cashier's check in the amount of $250,000 made out to her. Holly is flabbergasted. She looks at the men. One says, "Forget about the lawsuit and it's yours." They release the elevator. The doors open. They step out.

Fordham library. Holly's showing Nolan the check. She says she can use the money. Nolan says, "Shouldn't this be proof that I'm telling the truth?" She thinks about it. Yes. He's right. But she *needs* the money. Rattles off the reasons. Says she's sorry. She's taking the money. She leaves. Nolan is distraught.

Holly enters her bank. Sees a huge line. She has to pick up Scott. She can't wait. CUT TO: Holly on a bus, heading to Scott's school. She's staring at the $250,000 check. She daydreams about quitting her paralegal job, going to college full time, Scott attending private school, etc.

The bus stops outside Scott's school. Holly gets off. She walks fast to the front entrance where other parents are waiting for their kids. Introduces herself as Scott's mother.

Upon learning who she is, the parents start criticizing Scott, saying that his remarks about Santa Claus have caused havoc in their homes. Holly learns that Scott told all the kids that Santa Claus is real and that elves are real. One parent says her kid's having nightmares about elves. Another says she told her daughter Santa Claus doesn't exist when she was five and now she believes and feels conflicted.

Suddenly these yuppie parents are arguing about Santa Claus, whether he exists or doesn't. Holly sees that there is a clear delineation of opinions on the subject of Santa Claus. She says, "What would you all do if he really exists?"

They stare at her in silence, as if she's nuts. *And it's at this moment that Holly has an epiphany.*

The school doors open. The kids come out. Scott runs to Holly.

She asks if he still wants to sue Santa Claus. He says yes. She calls Nolan. Says she's changed her mind, but adds that she wants to get involved. Nolan says fine. Holly says that if he wants to come over for dinner they can start talking strategy.

She hangs up, then tears up the $250,000 check and tosses it in a trash can. PULLBACK REVEALS that the two chubby guys are watching. They don't look pleased. FURTHER PULLBACK shows Red Beret taking it all in.

That night at dinner Nolan gives Holly and Scott more information. "The hard part will be serving papers to Santa Claus. He's insulated by so many layers of protection from lawyers, accountants, and security. And the biggest problem of all is that nobody except little kids think he's real."

Holly asks, "Does anybody besides *you* know that Santa Claus is real?" Nolan explains that in the hundred-plus years since the 1892 Santa law suit there are only a handful of people who know and they're divided into two camps: those who *want* to get the truth out and those who *don't*. "And those of us who *want* to get the truth out are dwindling. Those who know the truth are reindeer breeders, Christmas tree farmers, and the ancestors of elves who left the North Pole."

It's Scott's bedtime. After a goodnight handshake from Nolan, Holly tucks Scott in. It's time for Nolan to go. At the door, Holly says she doesn't know why, but she's starting to accept the fact that not only Santa Claus but elves too *might* be real.

Holly at work. She surprises her friend Sylvia by saying she met a man that she could like. Sylvia pushes for information. It all sounds good. "Any drawbacks?" asks Sylvia. "Just one," says Holly. "His ancestry."

Various shots of the two chubby guys digging up information on Holly. And always hovering in the background is Red Beret, taking notes. Nolan Sr. meets with Red Beret to tell him he's figured out what's going on: "Here's my plan."

SERIES OF SCENES in which Nolan, Holly, and Scott work on the case. Scott likes being around Nolan. Holly takes this in. Nolan explains that the elves are the key to the case. He says that so much time has passed that the ones who know they're elves are few and they're dying out. His grandfather knew of two who are willing to testify.

"We have to get to them." Nolan says his grandfather was in his eighties when he died. "So are these two elves. Time is running out. Once we get them on board we can file our suit against Santa Claus. Without them as witnesses, we don't have a case."

"What do we do, go to the North Pole?" jokes Holly. "He's not at the North Pole. That's a ruse. The man in red hates cold weather. He likes warm weather. He has four homes. Two in California. Santa Monica on the beach and another in the northern wine country, Santa Rosa. Another in New Mexico, Santa Fe. And the fourth is his estate in Santa Catarina in Brazil.

Nolan says he'd like to use the time before Christmas to make their move. "It's Santa's busiest time. We can catch him off guard. We have to serve him the papers ourselves." Holly says that both she and Scott will be on holiday break. She adds that she's owed some time off at work.

MEANWHILE: Elliot Blitzer and the two chubby guys are plotting to interfere with their plans. He's listening to every telephone conversation Nolan has and, because of the bug planted in Nolan's apartment, he knows everything they're doing.

With Scott in tow, Nolan and Holly set out to find the first aged elf on Nolan's grandfather's list. They pile into Nolan's car and take off. We learn that elves require cold weather climates and that the vast majority lived in the Northeast. The first address is in Vermont.

During the trip Holly and Nolan get to know each other better. Scott encourages this. They go to the old elf's address only to discover that he died. He was ninety-three. His only family is a sister-in-law who knows nothing about his being an elf. She looks at Nolan as if he's crazy.

They drive to the second elf's address in New Hampshire. He's eighty-eight. Lives with his daughter and her family. His nine-year-old great-granddaughter sits by his side during the interview. She dotes on him. He's sick. His memory is going. For the last few months he's been telling people he's an elf. Everyone thinks he's delusional. Nolan knows his testimony would be useless.

They leave and are about to drive off when the old elf's great-granddaughter approaches them. She tells Nolan and Holly that the old elf gave her an envelope and told her to give it to whoever came around asking questions about Santa Claus. Nolan asks the kid what her great-grandfather said and she says, "That the truth will be found in the trees." What trees? The little girl doesn't know.

The envelope contains the name and address of *another* elf named Angus. Nolan has no memory of his grandfather ever bringing up *this* name. The address is in Maine. Directions are included. Nolan, Holly, and Scott follow them and arrive at a sprawling Christmas tree farm on the Canadian border.

They meet Angus. He looks ancient. They tell him how they came to find him, then they tell him about the Santa lawsuit. He's unfriendly and warns Nolan that if he persists in doing this it will change the course of his life. Nolan says he won't give up.

Then the old elf drops a bombshell: "The 1892 lawsuit is fraudulent. It had nothing to do with an elf being fired by Santa Claus because he was too tall. He was banished from the North Pole because he married Santa Claus's daughter. The baby that resulted from that union was Nolan's great-grandfather."

Which means that Nolan is the great-great-great-grandson of none other than... Santa Claus.

**!**

## ACT III

But the even bigger realization is that Nolan and his father are the only living descendents of Santa Claus. Nolan takes in the information. Now it's *his* turn not to believe.

Angus fills him in on what really happened. As he tells the story we'll FLASHBACK and *see* what he describes:

Nolan's great-grandfather, Eli, was born in 1892. His father was an elf named Ernie. Eli's mother was one of Santa Claus's daughters. It's forbidden for an elf to marry anyone except an elf. The crime is punishable by banishment from the North Pole

So Ernie was forced to leave. Santa's daughter stayed and gave birth to Eli, who was also banished and was raised in Maine by reindeer breeders who were trusted confidants of Santa Claus. They knew the truth about little Eli. They told no one. By the time Eli was twenty-one and was ready to go out into the world, the couple who raised him told him who he was. But they didn't tell him the exact truth. They only told him that his father was an elf and that he was fired by Santa Claus because he was too tall. They never mentioned to the young man that he was Santa Claus's grandson.

Eli wanted to meet his father. He tracked Ernie down and found him to be a broken man who blamed Santa Claus for all his problems.

Eli eventually married and had a son, Nolan's *grandfa-ther*, who was motivated to become a lawyer. But all his legal research resulted in dead ends.

*And we're back in the present.* Nolan says, "But that misin-formation ruined my grandfather's life." Angus nods soberly in agreement, then says, "Now that you know the truth, you have no reason to hold a grudge."

Nolan looks at Holly. She nods yes. "You've spent enough time on this." Nolan says, "Maybe my great-great-grandfather broke a rule by marrying Santa Claus's daughter, but Santa didn't also have to take it out on an innocent little baby."

Scott says, "Right", then stuns everybody. "It's one thing to get presents you didn't ask for and presents that don't work, but how could Santa let my daddy go away on Christmas Eve?"

Angus's cranky expression turns to one of compassion. Scott continues. "That's why I want to sue Santa Claus for malpractice. All I wanted for Christmas was for my daddy to come back and he never did."

Holly says, "That wasn't Santa's fault. It was daddy's fault."

Then Scott says it was mean for Santa to banish Nolan's great-great-grandfather from the North Pole. Angus says Santa Claus has always regretted that decision. Scott says, "If Santa Claus apologizes to Nolan I won't sue him for malpractice."

Holly's about to tell Scott to shush, when Angus says, "Maybe an apology is something Santa Claus would consider. Hold on." Angus takes out his cell and dials a number. He steps away. Talks softly into the phone. Hangs up.

"Nolan, in the interest of making things right with you — and to avoid being sued by you, Scott — Santa would like to issue you a formal apology. And since you're his great-great-great grandson, he'd like to do it in person so he can meet you." Angus says he'll arrange it after December 25th when things slow down. Angus says he'll be in touch.

Nolan, Scott, and Holly head back to New York. Nolan is in a daze. Scott asks Nolan if he can go with him when he meets Santa Claus. Holly says no. "That's between Nolan and Santa." Nolan wonders aloud what his father will think.

CUT TO: The Christmas tree field. Hiding behind one of the Christmas trees is Nolan's father, along with Red Beret. Nolan Sr. says, "This changes everything." Nolan Sr. is genuinely moved by what he's heard. PULLBACK REVEALS the two chubby guys watching.

Nolan, Scott, and Holly drive back to New York. They stop to stay overnight in a motel. Holly and Scott in one room. Nolan in the next. Scott falls asleep. Holly goes next door where she and Nolan can speak alone. The main topic of conversation is that Nolan can't believe he's related to Santa Claus.

Nolan explains that when he was a kid and found out he was descended from elves, it took him a long time to believe it. But that he's descended from Santa Claus is just too unbelievable.

In a total reversal, Holly now believes. Nolan starts to question everything about his past. Then, frustrated with the way he's acting, she lectures him. It's as if she's a lawyer making closing statements to a jury. She makes excellent points, diffuses every argument he makes, and manages to convince Nolan that it's all true.

Nolan is blown away by her performance. He realizes she's right and thanks her. Then he says, "You're gonna be a great lawyer. Maybe when you pass the bar we can be partners?"

She goes to him. "I've waited a long time for something to believe in," she says. "And who would've thought it would be an elf... with connections?" They share their first kiss.

Back in New York. Holly is preparing for her final exams at Fordham. She needs time alone to study so she asks Nolan if he'll take Scott off her hands for a day. She wants to hole up in the Fordham library to do nothing but study, without a phone or possibility of any interruption.

Nolan says sure. He and Scott spend time doing guy things. We see how Scott yearns for a father. And we see that Nolan has a sweet way of handling Scott. (And why wouldn't he? He's descended from Santa Claus.)

Then Nolan gets an urgent phone call from Angus. Santa Claus is sick. He wants to meet with Nolan immediately. Angus says he can take Santa's private plane. A limo is on the way. Nolan says he'll be ready. He tells Scott that he has to take him home.

They call Holly, but she's turned off her cell phone. Scott doesn't have keys. They can't get in the apartment. Nolan leaves a message on Holly's answering machine that he's taking Scott with him to meet Santa Claus. Nolan and Scott are whisked away in the limo. Following them are Nolan Sr. and Red Beret. And following *them* are the two chubby guys.

LaGuardia Airport. As Nolan and Scott go through ticketing, Nolan Sr. and Red Beret buy two tickets to Santa Catarina.

SANTA CATARINA. Nolan and Scott are met at the airport by a cheerful local who drives to a secluded estate on the water. Following close behind are Nolan Sr. and Red Beret.

They arrive at Santa Claus's estate. Go inside. They're looking forward to meeting Santa. Nolan remarks that it's exciting to be meeting his great-great-great-grandfather and how cool it is to know that it's Santa Claus.

Scott, unforgiving to the end, still feels Santa has some explaining to do. They're led out to the beach where they see a chaise lounge facing the water. Someone's sitting in it. They approach with anticipation.

It's Angus. He looks sad and upset. Plans have to be made. What plans? For Santa's successor. "Every 150 years a new Santa must take over the job. The only direct descendents left are Nolan and his father."

Nolan Sr. and Red Beret approach. Nolan Jr. quickly explains the situation. Angus says soberly, "One of you has to take over for Santa." Nolan Sr. is speechless.

They all go to Santa's bedroom. He's in bed, propped up with several pillows. He has that ageless, timeless look. He welcomes Nolan Sr. and Nolan Jr. He apologizes for banishing their ancestor from the North Pole those many years ago. "It was one of my bigger mistakes. Like when I gave Coca-Cola permission to use my face." They forgive him.

He gets to the business at hand. "One of you must carry on. Who will it be?" Nolan Jr. says no thanks. "I'm in love. I don't think I'd be very good at it." All eyes turn to Nolan Sr. He says yes, adding that he never liked being a lawyer and that he's always had a fondness for short people and reindeer.

Then Santa Claus turns to Scott. He tells him to get on the bed and sit on his lap. The gist of what he says is that even Santa Claus makes mistakes. Referring to Nolan, Santa whispers to Scott, "Maybe you'll get a new daddy next year." Scott smiles.

Then Santa Claus says, "There's only one thing left to do." He gestures to Angus who goes to a closet and removes — *a Santa suit*. Which he hands to Nolan Sr. Angus says, "Christmas is less than a week away. You'll have to start immediately." Nolan Sr. nods.

## SUPER – ONE YEAR LATER

**CHRISTMAS EVE**

Central Park. New York City. We find Scott, Nolan, and Holly sitting on a large boulder overlooking the lake. Scott's looking at the stars. "Where is he?" Scott asks. "It's time."

Holly looks at her watch. "Thirty seconds to go." Then Scott says, "There he is!" They look up. Flying in the night sky is a sleigh with eight reindeer. It's being flown by Nolan Sr. in full Santa Claus regalia. Sitting to his left is Red Beret, dressed like an elf. Nolan Sr. says, "Okay. We're over Central Park. When I say three... do it." Red Beret nods. "One, two, three!"

CUT TO: The control panels of the sleigh. They're ultra high tech. Red Beret presses a button, then — a jet stream shoots out and spells out...

Merry Christmas to Scott, Holly, and Nolan

Holly and Nolan, now married, kiss. They all wave. Then, with lightning speed, the sleigh and reindeer swoop down to where Scott, Holly, and Nolan stand. Suddenly, a ramp appears and the three of them run onto the sleigh. The sleigh then swoops back into the air.

The sleigh, loaded with presents. It's bigger than you'd think. Scott, Holly, and Nolan sit in the back. A friendly elf goes to Scott. Gives him a present.

Scott opens the present. It's a framed photograph of Santa Claus with the following inscription:

*To My Great-great-great-great Grandson Scott,*

*Now that Nolan has adopted you, it means that you're related to me. One day, if you choose to, I hope you'll consider continuing in the "family business."*

*Love, S. C. (Great-great-great-great Gramps)*

Scott smiles confidently, happily. He sits back. Clutches the photograph to his chest and enjoys the ride over Manhattan.

**The End**[†]

---

[†]Registered. WGA, East

# Strategy

## You and Your Relationship with Movies

If you're going to write movies you have to watch movies. But you have to look at them for more than entertainment. From now on, watching movies has to include study, research, and analysis.

I teach comedy writing and writing for television, as well as screenwriting. My students are required to write an episode of a sit-com currently on the air. I announce that this is the only course they'll take where they are required to watch TV.

The remark always gets a big laugh. The class thinks I'm kidding, but I'm not. Most of the people taking the course have an interest in becoming comedy writers, but outside of a few shows that they watch regularly for entertainment, they don't really study what they're watching. This is what separates the typical viewer from the person who wants to learn how to write for television.

# Viewing Exercise

I urge potential comedy writers to watch as many sit-coms as they can. Great ones, good ones, even lousy ones. I urge them to study the rhythms, beats, number of scenes, number of laughs per scene, length of scenes, and other distinctive factors they notice.

The same thing applies to screenwriters. Watch movies every chance you get. Good ones, bad ones, Indies, mainstream, new movies and old, genres you love, genres you hate.

But don't just watch them. Discover them. Examine them. Dissect and analyze why some work and some don't. Close scrutiny will reveal why some are great and others are so-whats or never-should-have-beens.

CHAPTER 20

# The Completed Process: Vague Idea, Treatment to Screenplay

*"And now I have finished a work that neither the wrath of love, nor fire, nor the sword, nor devouring age shall be able to destroy."*

— Ovid

I had a *vague idea*: what if a little kid wanted to sue Santa Claus? I wrote a short *outline*, then a detailed *treatment*. I could have gone from *outline* to *screenplay*, but since I had a producer interested in seeing something fast, I knew it would take me less time to do a *treatment*. Then I wrote the *screenplay* in one week.

Here are the first several pages to demonstrate how I moved on to the screenplay from the treatment. You'll see that I made a few name changes. Why? For no other reason than I thought the new names sounded better.

## *Dashing Through the Snow*

FADE IN ON
The face of Santa Claus. It fills the screen.

Specifically, the classic drawing of Santa by Thomas Nast with a flowing white beard, blustery red cheeks, bright eyes, and a glowing smile.

                    SUPER - ONE WEEK BEFORE CHRISTMAS
                              LOS ANGELES

Suddenly —

Something flies into frame and nails Santa on the nose. It's chocolate pudding. It oozes over his lips and beard.

A beat, then the hands of a child start smearing the pudding all over Santa's face.

PULLBACK TO REVEAL that we're in an elementary school hallway and a feisty seven-year-old boy is the culprit.

From the smile on his face, he's pleased with what he's done.

Meet SCOTTY THISTLE.

Think Jack Black in second grade.

INT. SCHOOL HALLWAY - DAY

Scotty is ready to launch another chocolate pudding bomb when —

A hand grabs his right arm. It's a teacher catching him in the act.

INT. ANOTHER HALLWAY - DAY

The teacher, her hand holding on to Scotty's right ear, marches him down the hall into...

INT. PRINCIPAL'S OFFICE - DAY

Scotty sits across from the PRINCIPAL, a woman in her fifties. The teacher who caught him is also there.

Scotty appears to be unfazed.

> PRINCIPAL
> Why did you throw pudding
> at Santa Claus, Scotty?

> SCOTTY
> Because I hate him.

> PRINCIPAL
> Why? When I was your age I
> loved Santa.

> TEACHER
> So did I. My sister and I
> would leave cookies for him.

> SCOTTY
> I tried that. Didn't work.
> I hate him because he doesn't
> keep his promises.

The principal and teacher look at each other, concerned.

> PRINCIPAL
> How do you mean?

> SCOTTY
> He never brings me the present
> he says he will. And the stuff he
> does bring breaks.

The principal refers to an open file on her
desk with Scotty's name on it.

> PRINCIPAL
> I see this is the third year
> in a row that you've become
> disruptive at school before
> Christmas. Last year you were
> caught...

QUICK FLASHBACK TO LAST YEAR

Scotty stands in a playroom at the school
with large drawings of Santa's reindeer.
He's crossing out their faces with crayons.

BACK TO SCENE

> PRINCIPAL
> And the year before that you...

QUICK FLASH BACK TO 2 YEARS AGO

Scotty is toppling over the sleigh set up in
the school yard.

BACK TO SCENE

> PRINCIPAL
> You give me no choice other
> than to call your mother.

Scotty is unsettled as the principal reaches
for her phone.

INT. LAW OFFICE - DAY

HOLLY THISTLE, Scotty's mom, thirtyish,
is at her desk at a law firm where she's a
full-time paralegal.

Attractive, but not overly stylish. Dressed
simply, inexpensively. She has a framed
picture of Scotty on her desk. As we'll
learn, she's taking night classes, studying
to be a lawyer.

Her phone rings. She answers it.

                    HOLLY
          (into phone)
          This is Holly Thistle....
          Yes.... Not again.

Holly shakes her head in frustration.

INT. COFFEE BAR - DAY

NOLAN ELWAY, thirty, stands in a short line.
Hyper, but sweet and good-natured.

Nearby two baristas are putting up Christmas
decorations. One takes some mistletoe and
proceeds to hang it over a doorway.

Nolan watches them. He looks upset.

                    BARISTA #1
          I always wondered how this kissing
          under mistletoe got started.

                    BARISTA #2
          I think it began in Italy.
          By shepherds or gondoliers
          or something.

                    CUSTOMER
          No. Belgium. It was a gypsy custom.

NOLAN

Actually, kissing under the mistletoe
began with the Greek festival of
Saturnalia and later with primitive
marriage rites. In Scandinavia,
mistletoe was considered a plant
of peace, under which enemies could
declare a truce or warring spouses
kiss and make up. In eighteenth
century England they had the
Kissing Ball, which they credited
with a magical appeal. At
Christmas-time a young girl
standing under a ball of mistletoe
brightly trimmed with evergreens,
ribbons, and ornaments could not
refuse to be kissed. Such a kiss
could mean deep romance, lasting
friendship, and good will. If no
one kissed a girl, she could not
expect to marry the following year.

Everyone stares at Nolan.

BARISTA #1

How'd you know all that?

NOLAN

You'd be surprised how much I know
about Christmas tradition. And it's
all bogus! (steps to counter)
Double decaf cappuccino.

INT. PRINCIPAL'S OFFICE - DAY

Holly sits across from the principal. In the
background, through a large window, we see
Scotty sitting alone in the outer office.

Scotty's file is open on the principal's
desk. She removes a drawing from the file
and holds it up.

It's a childlike drawing of Santa, but the
words SANTA CLAUS have been transformed into —

SATAN CLAWS

And Santa is drawn to look like the devil.

                PRINCIPAL
      We found it in his coloring book.

Holly looks at the drawing. Shakes her head
in embarrassment.

                PRINCIPAL
      Scotty is an excellent student.
      A popular boy. Respectful to teachers.
      But this is the third year in a row
      that he, well, seems to change as
      the holidays approach.

                HOLLY
      My husband and I divorced three
      years ago. Scotty took it hard.
      Especially around Christmas. That's
      when his father left.

The principal nods, understanding.

EXT. SCOTTY'S SCHOOL - DAY

Holly and Scotty are leaving the building.
She's laying into him.

HOLLY
You're behaving like a little Scrooge.
Refusing to sing Christmas carols,
defiling the picture of Santa Claus,
telling everyone that Santa is related
to Osama Bin Laden.

Scotty says nothing.

INT. ELWAY & ELWAY LAW OFFICES - DAY

Nolan enters the family-owned law firm where
he works as a lawyer. Two secretaries are
there.

SECRETARY #1
Are you looking forward to the
Christmas party Thursday night,
Nolan?

NOLAN
I don't do Christmas. Besides,
I won't be here.

He keeps walking.

SECRETARY #1
Why wouldn't he be here for the
Christmas party?

SECRETARY #2
You weren't here last year.
Never ask Nolan about Christmas.
He leaves town every year so he
doesn't have to celebrate the
holidays.

SECRETARY #1
Why?

                    SECRETARY #2
        No one knows.

EXT. SCHOOL PARKING LOT - DAY

Holly and Scotty walk to her car, a late
model Chevy.

                    HOLLY
        It's humiliating for me to get
        a call from the principal. I had
        to leave work early, which means
        I don't get paid for the time I
        missed. We need every penny,
        Scotty. And I had to bring work
        home tonight.

INT. HOLLY'S CAR - TRAVELING - DAY

Holly is still reprimanding Scotty.

                    HOLLY
        Tonight I was planning on studying
        for my exam at school. So because
        of what you did I'll be up all night,
        which means in the morning I'll be
        exhausted.

Scotty now feels guilty.

                    SCOTTY
        I'll help you study.

                    HOLLY
        That's sweet of you, honey,
        but I really need to cram.

                    SCOTTY
        You help me study. Let me help you.

She gives him a look. All is forgiven.

> HOLLY
Okay.

She pulls into their driveway. We see their house. A small bungalow. Needs a paint job. The yard is so-so.

From outside we see a Christmas tree in the window.

INT. HOLLY & SCOTTY'S HOUSE/LIVING ROOM – DAY

Modestly furnished. A makeshift desk consisting of two file cabinets and a sheet of plywood is Holly's work area. On it is the family computer, an old Mac.

A dining area is off the living room. Holly and Scotty eat dinner.

> HOLLY
I'm so relieved that the fall semester is ending.

> SCOTTY
So grown-ups like it when school ends too?

> HOLLY
(she chuckles)
I love school. I'm happy it's almost over because it means I only have two more years to go before I can become a lawyer.

> SCOTTY
You're gonna be the best lawyer ever in the history of the world.

Holly smiles.

INT. HOLLY & SCOTTY'S LIVING ROOM - NIGHT

Holly sits on the couch. Scotty sits across
from her holding a law textbook. They've
been at it for awhile. He's been picking a
term, she's giving the definition.

> SCOTTY
> Negligence.

> HOLLY
> Failure to exercise the care
> toward others which a reasonable or
> prudent person would do.

> SCOTTY
> Perfect.
> (he reads the next word)
> Malpractice.

> HOLLY
> An act which does not meet the
> standard of professional competence.

Scotty looks confused.

> SCOTTY
> Mom, what's the difference between
> negligence and malpractice.

> HOLLY
> Malpractice is more like incompetence.

> SCOTTY
> What's incompetence?

> HOLLY
> Not doing something very well. For
> example, I'm incompetent when I try
> to cook. You're incompetent at
> keeping your room clean.

Scotty smiles, but from the look on his face he gets an idea.

INT. SCOTTY'S ROOM - NIGHT

A typical kid's room. Toys. Trains. Holly tucks Scotty into bed. She kisses him good-night.

> SCOTTY
> Mom, when you become a lawyer, can I hire you?

> HOLLY
> (laughs)
> Of course. But why would you need a lawyer?

> SCOTTY
> I want to sue Santa Claus for malpractice.

Holly is taken aback.

> HOLLY
> Sweeties, you can't sue Santa Claus.

> SCOTTY
> Why not?

Holly is about to say, "Because he doesn't exist," but catches herself.

She decides to placate him.

> HOLLY
> Tell you what: When I become a lawyer I'll sue Santa Claus if you still want me to.

Scotty smiles and gives the right-arm pump signal and says a big —

                    SCOTTY
     Yes!

                    HOLLY
     Night, honey.

Holly turns on the nightlight and leaves.

CLOSE ON SCOTTY'S FACE as we CUT TO:

SCOTTY'S FANTASY

We're in a huge Victorian courtroom à la
Harry Potter with three stern-looking judges
wearing wigs and traditional British robes
holding court.

Santa Claus sits in the witness chair in
full costume.

Scotty and Holly sit at the lawyer's table.
They too are dressed as nineteenth-century
magistrates.

Holly, looking confident and strong, is
cross-examining Santa Claus.

                    HOLLY
     Did you not give Scotty Thistle
     what he wanted for Christmas?

                    SANTA CLAUS
     Yes.

                    SCOTTY
     I object! He said he'd bring me
     PlayStation 4 and he didn't!

                    ALL 3 JUDGES
     He didn't?

```
All three judges simultaneously bang their
gavels down and proclaim —
                    ALL 3 JUDGES
          Guilty!!!

Santa Claus cowers.

Scotty makes a face at Santa.

BACK TO SCOTTY IN HIS BEDROOM

Scotty smiles, then from the look on his
face, we get the feeling he's up to some-
thing.†
```

Ninety-four pages later, my initial vague idea resulted in a completed script. From first draft to final draft, four months. And I was fortunate enough to get a deal.

# Strategy

## One Thing and One Thing Only

Once you get past subplots, twists, turns, wrinkles and reversals, character histories, and all the other stuff, a story is ultimately about one thing and one thing only. The forward dramatic movement of your main character trying to get what he wants and either succeeding or failing. If he succeeds, the story might continue further showing the positive or negative results of getting what he wanted. If he fails, the story might continue further showing the positive or negative results of *not* getting what he wanted. Or, if he gets what he set out to get, the story will end.

---

†Registered, WGA, East

# Writing Exercise

Practice writing dialogue by writing a two-character ten-minute play. Fill it with long monologues. In a play you're allowed to have monologues. In a screenplay they should be avoided unless they come at a point in the script (usually in the third act) when they serve to deliver an emotional payoff for a character.

CHAPTER 21

# Adaptation

*"A movie is not a book. If the source material is a book, you cannot be too respectful of the book. All you owe to the book is the spirit. Everything else, just tear that motherfucker apart."*

— Richard Price

There are a couple of dozen novels I've read that I would've loved to adapt into a screenplay. Most of them already have been or are in one stage or another of development. Whether they'll get made or not is another story. One of my favorite novels is *Time and Again*, by Jack Finney. From the first time I read it, I knew it was destined for the big screen.

I was once in a meeting with a producer and the subject of adaptation came up. He asked me if there was any particular book that I would like to turn into a screenplay. I immediately told him *Time and Again*. He smiled and said, "Join the club." He then proceeded to tell me that a number of directors have been trying to get a movie of *Time and Again* off the ground virtually since its publication in 1970. He then told me that numerous name screenwriters had already written spec scripts on the book just to be involved. As of this writing, it still hasn't been made.

Often, once a screenwriter or playwright is hot, he'll be in a position where a studio or major producer asks him what he'd like to do next. This is where he can use his newfound clout to get a job writing a screenplay based on a novel or screenplay written by some other writer.

I don't recommend beginning your screenwriting career by doing an adaptation of someone else's work. You're taking someone else's story, characters, dialogue, and, well, all of his creativity.

Make your initial bones with your own original idea. Blow away agents, managers, and producers with your own creativity. Once you've duly impressed the right people with your writing, then take on an adaptation.

Let's say you've reached that stage and there's a novel or play that you want to adapt. How do you do it?

I was involved in the film version of *Spinning Into Butter,* a wonderful play by Rebecca Gilman, starring Sarah Jessica Parker and released in 2009. The play had a single set and seven characters. The first step was to "open it up," which means I had to take the story out of the stage setting.

I began by doing a treatment. I chose not to do an outline because the play existed. I'd seen it and read it. Doing a short outline wasn't necessary. My intention was to follow the storyline of the play as closely as possible. A treatment was the best approach.

At its core, adaptation is all about making choices. Specifically, which characters need to be expanded, eliminated, minimized, or created. So I had to look at the play and figure out the choices I needed to make.

The play is about a racial incident at a small college in New England. The victim is an eighteen-year-old freshman, African American, who is never seen in the play, only referred to. My first choice was that this character had to be in the screenplay. He didn't necessarily require a big part, but the audience needed to see him. It would help them identify with him. Similarly, in the play, the racial incident is only referred to. I felt that an audience needed to see it take place.

So the first thing I wrote in the treatment was a scene late at night on the campus. Suddenly, a pair of boots comes into frame. We follow the character wearing them to the entrance of a dorm. Inside the dorm, the character approaches a room and posts a racial slur on the door.

That was the *instigating event*. And it created two questions: Who did it and why? So the movie has begun. Next, Sarah Jessica Parker's character had to be introduced, be informed of the incident, then be seen taking steps to handle it. That entailed her meeting other students and officials at the college. These officials were in the play, in that one room, but there had to be more scenes with them outside that room. So the treatment showed how opening up the setting would be handled.

I had to make a decision about the romantic subplot of the play. There was an intricate romance between the main character, her boyfriend, and a new woman in his life. Should I keep it or not?

In the play there was an absence of college students, save for one boy whose storyline was an important subplot germane to the theme of the play. It was also the basis for a powerful scene in the play. It could be kept untouched. But as this was a movie taking place on a college campus, we needed to see students. So situations in the play that were only talked about were now scenes. There was a student rally that played an integral part of the film.

In the play, the single set served the purpose of the play. A film could've been made without opening the play up, but it wouldn't have been as interesting. It would have been essentially a filmed play. Those seldom work.

It's unnecessary for me to go through the step-by-step process I used to finish my adaptation. Once my adaptation was finished, the author of the play did a draft, then it went straight to script. Subsequently, another writer was brought on who made additional changes and embellishments resulting in a shooting script.

All you need to understand is that when you've been hired to do an adaptation of someone else's completed work, it's incumbent upon you to respect the material. If you need to eliminate characters and/or plot points, make sure you're not harming the story. The same goes if you need to add or alter a character.

Some projects are easier to adapt than others. Adapting *The DaVinci Code* had to be a nightmare. The book had a great story, but the charm of the book was all the information Dan Brown provided on the history of religion, art, and symbols. Most of that couldn't be in the movie. Why not? Because it would slow down the dramatic tension.

Same with *Angels and Demons*. Another great story filled with lots of information about the Catholic Church. The movie version, as with *The DaVinci Code*, was basically a bare-bones thriller. Fast-paced, pretty much a thrill a minute, murders, betrayal. Nowhere near as entertaining or satisfying as the novel, because a movie is about streamlining and moving the story forward.

Could I have done a better job of adapting either novel to the screen? Hell, no. No one could've done a faithful adaptation of that book and many others without churning out a talkie 400-page script.

Adaptation is a challenge. Somebody has to decide what's going to stay and what must go. As the person doing the job, you'll make the first choices.

Make sure you've thought your story through. Know where all the pivotal plot points come. Know where the act-breaks fall.

# Writing Exercise

Find a short story that you like and turn it into a 30-page screenplay. *Brokeback Mountain* was a short story that first appeared in *The New Yorker*.† Read it. It wasn't especially long, but it was turned into a full-length screenplay. See what you can do in 30 pages with another story.

---

†October 13, 1997

# PART 2
# CHARACTER-IZATION

■ ■ ■

*"Truth does not blush."*

— Quintus Septimius Tertullianus

CHAPTER 22

# Getting Reacquainted with Who You Are and Where You've Been

*"Strong reasons make strong actions."*

— William Shakespeare

Which came first, the chicken or the egg? Here's a tougher question: which comes first, character or plot?

It depends.

Some people come up with a powerful story that can be plotted out fairly simply. Their particular hell will be in creating an interesting protagonist.

Others don't have the foggiest notion of a storyline, but have an intriguing main character. Finding the right plot to put this character in will be what keeps them up nights screaming.

Given my druthers, I'd rather have the story and worry about a protagonist later, simply because it's easier to construct a character than a storyline.

Easier. Hah!

Let me get something out in the open: Whenever I describe something as being "easier," I don't mean that literally. From this moment on, when I use the word "easier," I really mean "slightly less difficult."

Constructing a character is looking first at yourself, then at everybody else. The best way to look at yourself is to get in touch with the less-than-flattering sides to your personality.

Why?

I know that Mother Teresa was kind, loving, and charitable to everyone she encountered. A true saint on earth.

But that's not dramatic. It's just, well, nice.

It would be more interesting to know that she was a closet fan of *True Blood*, relaxed by reading Stephen King novels, and liked to pig out on Ring Dings.

## Writing Exercise

Answering the following questions will help you get reacquainted with who you are and where you've been. Try writing your answers in longhand rather than typing them. You'll take more time to think them through. I encourage you to be brutally honest.

1) What is the worst thing that ever happened to you?
2) What are the three biggest regrets of your life?
3) Who or what would you die for?
4) What is the worst thing you've ever done?
5) Who are you prejudiced against?

You may be wondering how the answers to any or all of these question will help you start a screenplay.

Welcome to the world of character development. The first character you're going to "develop" is you.

Let's use question No. 1 as an example.

Did the "worst thing that ever happened to you" come to mind instantly, or did you have to think about it? Did you have a hard time pinpointing only one event? Were there two or three things (or more) that could qualify as "worst?" Did digging into such painful territory make you ill at ease? Did you remember something you had blocked out for years? Did something you previously thought of as the worst thing that ever happened to you change as you thought about it?

Because I was only thirteen when I lost my father, for years I thought of his death as the worst thing that ever happened to me. But twenty-two years later, the production of a play of mine, slated to open on Broadway, was cancelled when the financial backing fell apart. Because by then I had come to terms with the loss of my father, this blow to my career seemed most devastating.

I couldn't write for months. I went into a depression. It took nearly a year to get over it. It made me less trusting of people, especially producers.

Several years later my dog, Putney, died. He'd been a part of my life for more than seventeen years — four years *longer* than my father. Was his death the worst thing that ever happened to me? No. But it was one of the most painful things I ever had to get through and I know I'll feel the loss forever. I also know that, at some point, I'll write about it. How many experiences in your life are really screenplays waiting to happen?

The point of the questions is to see how honest and open you can be *to yourself.*

If you're introspective and self-analytical by nature, my guess is that you'll have an easier time writing down the truth. If you have a "get over it" personality, you may have a harder time recalling things because you've put them behind you.

But since you want to be a writer, dredging up the old pain might turn into a unique resource for you.

The purpose of these exercises is to force you not to play games with your characters. The worst thing any screenwriter can do is write superficial, one-dimensional characters who bear no resemblance to human beings. You've seen movies populated with characters like that.

They're tiresome and dull.

Give your protagonist shadings and contours, internal and exterior conflicts. Self-doubt and false confidence are two good ones. Maybe a behavior-altering incident: As a result of someone's pathological lateness, a loved one dies. The death serves as a catalyst to the person being overly conscious about being on time.

And family secrets are always fun. The gay uncle in Detroit who's sixty-four and has lived with his "roommate" for the last thirty-eight years. The grandmother everyone pretends is dead, but is really in prison for murdering grandpa and his mistress way back when. The black sheep brother who is married with four kids, but maintains a "second family" on the other side of town.

Look into yourself. Then look into the histories of the people you know best.

Try to remember all the confidences and secrets you've been told. Then give them to your characters. As you develop the protagonist of your screenplay, answer the five questions from his or her point of view. It will serve as a solid starting point.

Because you have your screenwriting notebook, no one but you will know how you answered these questions. No one will judge you.

Let's use question No. 2 as another example. Two people, two different answers.

PERSON A

"The three biggest regrets of my life are that I never learned to ski, I never went to Disneyland, and I never asked Joe Montana for his autograph when I had the chance."

PERSON B

"The three biggest regrets of my life are that I married a man I didn't love because I was pregnant, I didn't have an abortion, and I didn't get a divorce because he was rich."

One person's answers were fairly superficial while the other person answered from deep within herself.

Does it mean that Person A had no profound regrets? Maybe. Maybe not. He could be in denial, hiding his childhood, or protecting himself from some long ago pain. Or maybe the three regrets he listed are all he's capable of handling. Or maybe he's one of those rare folks who sails through life without anything tragic happening to him, so his regrets would indeed be less complex.

But with both of these people, a character is taking shape. One might have more depth, but the other might be more fun to be around.

The object is to come up with an interesting, appealing character and then to put him or her into an interesting, compelling story.

Through subsequent chapters we'll continue to work on character. Simultaneously, we'll work on the story you want to tell. And as we proceed to the next step, I want you to take your answer to question No. 4 — What is the worst thing you've ever done? — and expand on it.

For example, you might answer:

"The worst thing I ever did was have sex with my best friend's fiancée three days before their wedding."

BRIEF EXPANSION

My best friend was the type who always got the prettiest girls. He fancied himself a ladies' man and liked to brag about all the girls he slept with. But he vowed that the girl he married would be a virgin. When he met Gina, he told me that it was love at first sight and that he was the first guy she slept with. I liked Gina and I felt she liked me. I considered her almost like a sister. Three nights before the wedding I had to drop something off at Gina's house. She invited me in for a drink and the next thing I knew we were having sex. Afterwards, she told me that she wanted to get even with my best friend because of all the girls he'd slept with. I never told him what happened. Nine months later Gina had a baby. That was five years ago. The kid looks like me. My friend and I don't hang out anymore. He told me Gina doesn't like me.

What the *expansion* does is give more information about the events that led up to "the worst thing" this person ever did and the cause and effect of his action. A story is beginning to blossom. We know something has happened and that there were consequences, and it's easy to see how even more consequences can follow.

After you have completed the expansion of your answer to question No. 4, give yourself a pat on the back. You have just written your first storyline.

Creating storylines is a good habit to get into. You force yourself to think ahead.

But because thinking ahead is difficult, so too are storylines. I insist that my students learn how to write them. Some take to them quickly and naturally. Others despise them. I like to say that even if you intend never to do one again, it's good to know how to write a storyline because the day may come when a producer asks you for one.

It works like this: You've finished a script and somehow, either through an agent or your own hard work, you've gotten it onto the desk of a producer. It gets read and the producer calls you in and says she likes your screenplay and she likes your writing, but she doesn't want to make your movie.

She asks if you have any other ideas. This is where having a vague idea or two comes in handy.

Let's say you tell her your idea for a movie. And let's say she likes it. She will ask you for something on paper. One page or two or maybe more.

This is where knowing how to construct a storyline and "thinking ahead" comes in handy.

She doesn't want a full-length screenplay or half of one or even the first act. All she wants is that vague idea or basic premise you "pitched" her expanded so she can show it to someone else: her partner, an investor, her husband, her lover, another higher-ranking producer, a studio executive, or all of the above.

If you can deliver a solid storyline that gets across the big picture of the movie it can become, you're one step closer to a deal.

# Strategy

## People Are the Same Everywhere

In my travels, I've been exposed to enough people from different countries and cultures to believe that people are the same when it comes to the emotions and feelings that go with the territory of being human.

It's essential to know that the man in Paris or Tokyo feels just like us when his heart's been broken. Or that the woman in Munich whose husband is unjustly accused of a crime is in just as much turmoil as might be a woman in Dublin, Florence, or Mexico City.

Throughout the rest of the world, American movies are, ultimately, foreign films. Whether the European market likes American movies or American movie stars is a separate issue, but, even when the translation is through subtitles, "foreigners" are identifying with the stories told by American screenwriters.

Language, mores, and culture may be regional, but human emotions are universal. You're not writing for your neighborhood, you're writing for the world.

# Writing Exercise

Come up with a premise for a mystery set in the most exciting place you've ever been. If you've never been anywhere, go somewhere exciting, then do the assignment.

# CHAPTER 23

# How Did Your Main Character Get There?

*"Every man has a sane spot somewhere."*

— Robert Louis Stevenson

Like most adult males, I've seen my share of porn. Titillation aside, from the first skin flick I saw in high school I've been fascinated with one thing: How does somebody decide to have sex for pay and allow themselves to be filmed?

Is it economic? Is it because of a drug problem, which still makes it economic? Is it to have sex? Is it the indirect result of a screwed-up childhood? It's the same with rock stars, the more flamboyant ones in particular. When did Lady Gaga decide to dress that way?

Let's bring it down from porn actors and rock stars to your Uncle Norm, the accountant. How did he arrive at that position? With every new person I meet, I'm always fascinated with how he got into his line of work. There's always a reason. For example, your father was a CPA, so it seemed logical that you would be too.

How did you get your job? How did you meet your mate? How do you happen to be living where you're living? What lucky break gave you a leg up on everyone else? What bad break set you back five years? What did you do that came back to haunt you and ruined your career?

Does it seem that some people just sail through life, dodging bullets, avoiding tragedies, being lucky, making right choices, always having things go their way?

Knowing how and why your main characters got to where they are at the start of your screenplay is important.

That's why creating a history or backstory for your character can be important.

Like many of the processes discussed, some things work for some and don't for others. I know many people who hate doing character histories, choosing instead to begin writing only knowing a smidgen about the character and learning who she is and what she's all about as they get into the script. I'm like this. Writing character histories filled with detailed minutiae of a person's life doesn't make anything easier for me. I prefer to have a general idea of who my protagonist is and what she wants, then discover her as I churn out the pages.

I learn when I must make my character talk to the other characters. So may you. But I know many people who won't start writing until they've created a two- or three-page, single-spaced background for a character — and not necessarily the lead. Some actors are known for preparing histories for each character they play. Acting isn't just memorizing the words. It's understanding what they mean to the character.

Which is the reason screenwriters must make good choices.

If the playwright or screenwriter is around rehearsal, an actor has the option of asking questions about the history of a fictional character. The writer may have answers or may not. Or the answers may not "work" for the actor. The actor will then begin working on her own character history. Screenwriters can make choices too: Start writing and discover who your main character is as you go, do a sketchy outline of who she is, or do a painstakingly detailed history.

But whatever your choice, at some point you must ask yourself:

1) Who is this woman?

2) Where has she been?

3) What does she want?

4) Why does she want it?

5) What is she prepared to do to get it?

6) If she gets it, what will happen to her?

7) If she doesn't get it, what will happen to her?

8) What is her greatest flaw? Her greatest strength?

9) What does she fear the most?

10) What is her darkest secret?

Like eating sushi, rattlesnake stew, or steak tartar, you won't know if you like character histories until you try one. If it works for you, great. If it doesn't, try a more intuitive approach. Whatever you use should put you on an emotional parity with your characters.

# Strategy

## Pretend Your Screenplay Is a Cave and You're Walking in the Dark

Now pretend you're holding a flashlight. Turn it on and the beam might extend three feet. Walk those three feet and the beam extends three more feet, or five, six, or nine feet. That's what writing a script is like. You're in the darkness, then you see some light and you advance a few pages. Sometimes the beam is very bright. Sometimes it stays dark until you see a glimmer of light. Then you keep going. Light and dark. Finally, if you're lucky and you stay with it, you'll have a first draft.

# Writing Exercise

Make a list of every job (full- or part-time) you've ever had and write down the circumstances of how and why you got it. Apply that to how your main characters got where they are at the start of your screenplay.

CHAPTER 24

# Touchy-Feely and Warm and Fuzzy vs. Nasty, Bitchy, and Really Evil

*"Whoever fights monsters should see to it that in the process he does not become a monster."*

— Friedrich Nietzsche

Normal, happy, well-adjusted people with sunny dispositions and healthy outlooks on life are boring. Not necessarily in real life, but on the screen.

Any actor will tell you it's more fun to play the villain than the good guy. And most actresses would rather sink their teeth into the part of a bitchy, nasty shrew than the All-American girl, Super Mom, or kindly grandma with an apple pie baking in the oven.

Jack Nicholson's character, Melvin, in *As Good as It Gets* was reprehensible, unlikable, selfish, controlling, obsessive-compulsive, and a dozen other unseemly things as well. We disliked him so much we couldn't take our eyes off him. If in real life we lived next door to the character he portrayed, we would detest and avoid him and, most certainly, not find him to be intriguing to watch.

But spending two hours with Jack playing Melvin was fun, entertaining, moving, and ultimately satisfying. Was it Jack Nicholson's Oscar-winning performance that we liked or was it the part? With all due respect to Jack, I say it was the part. Dustin Hoffman, Al Pacino, Michael Douglas, Robert DeNiro, and maybe a dozen other actors could have done impressive things with that role primarily because the writers had created a complex, multi-dimensional character.

They could have made him a Caspar Milquetoast type, or maybe just a little obsessive-compulsive, or Walter Mitty, or a mama's boy, but they made him just nasty. And we loved it. Just as we love that old curmudgeon of a character called Scrooge. Or Bill Murray in *Scrooged*. Or Clint Eastwood in *Gran Torino*.

Not that I'm saying every protagonist has to be obnoxious, repulsive, hateful, or annoying. I can rattle off twenty-five movies where the main character was likable and sympathetic and identifiable.

BUT... something was wrong with them. They were nice people, but damaged. Totally screwed up! The point is, don't make your protagonist sugary sweet, too happy, too content, too unaware, or in denial of his/her problems.

Give your characters something dark that haunts them; maybe not every waking moment, but in the small hours of the night. Give your characters a demon. A weakness. A secret that, if ever revealed, would humiliate them.

Let the touchy-feely, warm and fuzzy people (assuming you know any) stay in your real life and keep them out of your screenplays.

# Strategy

## The Good Bad Guy

Give your hero a worthy opponent. The best James Bond movies have villains who are truly evil, yet interesting, charming, and strangely likable. If you step back and look at all the James Bond films, no matter who's playing James, the stories are really about the villains.

So-so villain, forgettable Bond film.

Great villain, great Bond film.

So don't be afraid to make your hero's opponent truly repugnant. It's more fun that way. If we know our hero will eventually encounter a wimp or a moderately bad guy, it's boring. But if we know our hero will confront someone who is intellectually and physically his equal, or — even better — his superior, the face-off becomes high drama.

# Writing Exercise

Make a list of your ten all-time favorite bad guys/gals in films. Then describe why they are so compelling.

CHAPTER 25

# Show Me, Don't Tell Me

*"The cruelest lies are often told in silence."*

— Robert Louis Stevenson

Actions speak louder than words. We all heard that for the first time in grade school. It's true in life and it's even more true in the writing of a screenplay.

The point is, if you make a big deal that your lead character is extremely skillful at something — say he's a great salesman, or she has the ability to throw together a gourmet meal out of a hodgepodge of random ingredients, or he's a coach who knows how to motivate his team with inspirational pep talks — *show* that salesman schmoozing the hell out of a prospect and *show* that woman putting a fabulous meal together and let's *see* that coach preparing his team for action.

Not only is it a more interesting way to further the plot, it's a whole lot better than hearing another character remark, "Ya know, that Sally knows how to cook awesome meals out of virtually nothing."

And if a character has a particular skill or ability that will come in handy much later on in the script, show your character utilizing that skill in a way that doesn't suggest how it will pay off later.

This "giving of information" is called exposition and the cousins of exposition are called preparation and foreshadowing.

Unlike a play or novel where words and time are more readily available to the writer, a screenplay can make an important point simply by showing a character in action without him — or anyone else — saying a single word.

Show me how much you love me, don't tell me.

Give me a pay raise, don't tell me how good I am and that I'll be rewarded soon.

Don't draw a line in the sand, then take no action when someone crosses it.

Actions speak louder than words.

Especially in screenplays.

# Strategy

## Make It Dirty, Then Clean It Up
## Until You Can Use It

Don't edit or censor yourself. If your script is running long (Act I ends on page 58, Act II is 97 pages, and the first draft comes in at 188 pages) don't sweat it. Get it all out. See what you've written. Worry about cutting it down to size later.

Same with risqué material. No matter how filthy something is, keep it. Don't stifle yourself. Censor yourself later. There are wonderful gems to be found when you let things happen and don't harness yourself with rules.

# Writing Exercise

Write a sex scene. Not raunchy or pornographic. But write a scene that begins with a couple making out, which leads them to lusty groping, after which they make their way to bed. Have them talking as they progress from kissing to sex. Do one version as if you're writing a comedy and another as if your scene is a drama.

CHAPTER 26

# That Which Does Not Kill You Makes You Stronger (and Gives You Story Ideas)

*"If you want to find out if you are lucky,*
*go to a craps game."*

— Gambler's Maxim

I know what it's like to face death. As I touched on earlier, a number of years ago I was robbed at gunpoint in my apartment. A few more details will paint the complete picture.

The only time I ever saw a gun close up was when I stared at the one being pointed in my face. More than anything the gun is uppermost in my mind. But if my life depended on it, I couldn't recognize it nor could I recognize the man who pointed it at me.

The police who came to investigate asked me if the gun was real. I didn't know. It *looked* real. It never occurred to me that it might not have been real. A toy? No way. It hadn't actually touched me anywhere, so I didn't feel the proverbial sting of cold metal against human flesh.

I tell the story of my mugging less often than I did during the first year and especially the first few weeks after it happened. In those days I spoke of it with an attitude of exuberance and even enthusiasm, almost as if I'd beaten cancer or death, which, in a sense, I felt I had. But inside, I was enraged. I played that down.

I only tell the story now in classrooms as an example of the worst thing that ever happened to me. When I tell it now there is little enthusiasm and even less rage. The telling has become rote for me. I feel like an actor who has played the same role for so long that he can phone in his performance. However, if my audience is receiving the story well, I can get into it. If the audience seems dulled or disinterested, I make my points and move on.

After telling the story for many years, I sometimes find myself questioning my accuracy and wondering if I'm unintentionally embellishing one fact or minimizing another. I often ask myself if a certain detail is too ironic or quirky or if something sounds too contrived or maybe even too Hollywood.

Did the man who stuck that gun in my face and held it on me for thirty-five minutes *really* pet my dog gently on the head? Yes. Did he *really* pour himself a glass of vodka and then offer me one? Yes. Did I actually have the nerve to ask him not to take my ring because it was a memento from my father? Yes. And after he took a hundred dollars and change from me, did I really have the balls to ask him for a subway token before he left? Yes.

There is nothing about that night that is hazy in my mind, starting at the precise moment the incident began: 7:40 p.m. I was meeting friends for dinner at 8:00 p.m. Being a stickler about arriving on time, I knew from previous visits to their house that it was exactly a twenty-minute walk, door to door. So at twenty-to-eight I walked out of my apartment, locked the door, and there he was.

He was black. Late thirties to early forties. He wore a white winter raincoat. He pulled the gun out of the right pocket of the raincoat and pointed it at my head. I saw him cock the hammer. I remember saying out loud, "Oh God," softly. Inside, I thought, "This is it."

He asked me if there was anyone in my apartment. I said no, except for my dog. He asked how big the dog was. I told him he was small, and, fearing for my dog's safety, made a point of saying that he was extremely friendly.

We went inside. The thirty-five minutes he was in my apartment seemed like three or four minutes. Never in my life before or since has time sped by so fast. I didn't look at the clock until he left. It was 8:15 p.m. I told him that the only cash I had was in my wallet, that I didn't keep money in the apartment. He told me to hand him the cash and dump my credit cards onto the floor. I wondered why but decided not to ask. I told him I had a savings passbook. He didn't want it. I volunteered that I had a checkbook. My offering him my checkbook resulted in the only light moment in the course of the robbery.

"What are you gonna do?" he asked with a gruff laugh and a smirk. "Write me a check?"

Besides the money, he ended up taking my wristwatch, a brand new cassette tape recorder and a valuable guitar.

Before he left he dismantled my telephone and took my keys. To my surprise he said that he would leave them downstairs. I didn't believe that he would. He did. They were on the second floor landing. The last words he said to me were that he had a friend watching downstairs and if I left the apartment in less than ten minutes he would come back and kill me.

Once he was gone the story becomes anti-climactic. The police came. They made it clear they couldn't do much. The robber wore gloves so there were no fingerprints. They said I was smart not to panic or fight him. A couple of days later I went to a police station to look over mug shots. The person I was convinced was my robber turned out not to be the man. The man I picked was already in jail. I kept looking at more mug shots, but after about two hours I gave up. Technically, other than filing the insurance claim, the mugging experience ended when I walked out the door of the precinct house.

But emotionally and psychologically, the experience didn't end. To this day I'm far more cautious than anyone I know. Not afraid. Not paranoid. Just cautious. I was lucky. I had a humane robber. I remember everything as if it were yesterday. But I often wonder if he still remembers it the way I do.

I doubt it.

But if there is anything for me to be grateful about what happened that night, it's that I had a new appreciation for life and, as a writer, I had experienced what it's like to taste my own mortality. When I write a character in the jaws of death, I'm not making up the emotions. I've lived them.

Which is why life experience is such a huge plus for a screenwriter. If you've never experienced something, you might *think* you know what it's like and you might do tons of research to get a *feel* of what it's like and if you have a vivid imagination you might be able to *guess* what it's like. But there's nothing like being in a plane that's nose-diving toward the ground and is seconds away from crashing — and then doesn't — to know what that particular horror (and thrill) must be like.

# Writing Exercise

Make a list of the five most difficult things you've done that made you a stronger, tougher, better person. Consider using those experiences to embellish your characters.

# Strategy

## It Never Gets Easier, But You'll Get Better

No matter how competent you become at completing the first draft of your screenplay, then going through all the machinations of rewriting and making it a terrific script, the next one you write will present the same problems, only they will be different. You'll know structure better, especially the value of having a powerful end-of-Act II event. You'll understand the impact of shorter, crisper dialogue and appreciate that in screenwriting less is truly more. You'll know that starting your story as soon as possible and letting the reader and audience know what your main character wants from the get-go is a huge plus.

# CHAPTER 27

# Public Lives, Private Lives, and Secret Lives

*"Everyone is a moon, and has a dark side which he never shows to anybody."*

— Mark Twain

Let's say that the persona we present to our friends, neighbors, and co-workers is living our public life and that the person we are at home — with our spouses, children, parents, and in-laws — is leading our private life.

So what's the deal with the secret life?

I personally know of two men who had second families in another part of the town in which they lived: the family of record with the wife, kids, house, and dog — and the girl-friend with the illegitimate child. Both men maintained two families. Guess which family they spent the holidays with?

Then there's the church-going, salt-of-the-earth guy next door, who works with youth groups, annually donates blood, dresses like a clown for charity, and spends weekends visiting old folks in senior citizen centers. And did I mention that he has a gorgeous wife and four beautiful kids? Well, he likes to wear his wife's clothes on weekends.

And, of course, there's the super-straight jock who's gay. Or the girl who dresses like a hooker and wears so much makeup you'd think she's a Mary Kay cosmetics saleswoman who radiates sexuality, but who's a virgin.

Speaking of virgins, I know of two women well past fifty who have never slept with a man. They're not lesbians. They're not asexual. They're heterosexual virgins. How I know this is not because they told me. It's just information I picked up from people close to them, revealed in confidence by someone who needed to share a bit of surprising information with someone who won't judge, but will say, "There's a story in there."

In extremes there are stories. The tale of the fifty-two-year-old virgin is as fascinating to me as the tale of the thirty-two-year-old porn star who finds religion after sleeping with four hundred guys. I know of a woman, a virgin until age forty-five, who finally slept with a guy. One time. And she got pregnant, which was her sole reason for never wanting to have intercourse.

I tell my students and clients to look for the drama in extreme situations. A man's first day on the job and his last day on the job after forty years are interesting. Why else are there so many stories about cops either at the end of their career or just starting out? A detective on the job for six years or fourteen years or even twenty-three years isn't as dramatic as the cop who has one week left before retirement and he's never killed anyone and he's put in a situation where he may have to.

That's dramatic.

I have an acquaintance from my youth who is a nun. She went into the convent at the age of sixteen. I don't know if she ever had a date with a boy. Perhaps she did. She was rather sheltered and overprotected by her parents. Her life experience was, to say the least, limited. I know of another woman who went into the convent after being married and having children. Of these two nuns, whose story would you rather watch in a theater?

If you said the latter, we agree. The tale of a woman who has experienced life, marriage, sex, giving birth, child-rearing, and all the problems and complexities that go with the territory would be far more dramatic when she makes a decision to become a nun. Imagine the obstacles. Aren't nuns supposed to be virgins and unwise to the ways of the world?

And human nature being what it is, the nuns that would be training this woman wouldn't necessarily welcome her with open arms. I had twelve years of Catholic education, eight of them being taught by nuns. I remember some of the nuns I knew as pleasant and kind women. I remember a few others as mean-spirited and angry. Women who probably didn't want to become nuns, but did so to please a parent. Women who shouldn't have stayed in the convent, but were afraid to leave for one reason or another.

Imagine a few — or just one — of these angry nuns encountering this woman who became a nun well past middle-age and had experienced marriage and sex and independence.

That's a story.

I think everyone has a secret life, even if it's bingeing on Three Musketeers bars in the middle of the night when the rest of the family is sleeping, or reinventing one's self in chat rooms on the Internet.

You know what your secret life is. I know what mine is. And I know about the secret lives of a few other people that I found out by accident, through gossip or from the person himself.

Odds are that you know about the secret lives of people. This is where you find the shapes and contours of a character. Not in the overt and obvious. But in the dark crevices.

# Strategy

## The First Five Times You Had Sex

If the first five flights you took almost crashed, odds are you're going to hate to fly. If the first five times you ate sushi it gave you food poisoning, there's all likelihood that you won't like raw fish. Oh yes, and if your first five sexual encounters were unpleasant or ugly — you see where I'm going? On the other hand, if your first five sexual, flying, and sushi-eating experiences were exhilarating, you're probably going to love doing all three as often as possible. My point is, creating rich, complicated characters means giving them strong reasons for their behavior.

# Writing Exercise

Make a list of five to ten things you disliked the first time you tried them, i.e., drinking alcohol, traveling, eating raw oysters. Perhaps some you still dislike, but others you now enjoy. Consider giving your dislikes to your characters to make them more three-dimensional.

# PART 3
# DIALOGUE AND CONFLICT

*"What comes easiest for me is dialogue. Sometimes when my characters are speaking to me, I have to slow them down so that I'm not simply taking dictation."*

— Richard Russo

■ ■ ■

*"It is easier to be a lover than a husband for the simple reason that it is more difficult to be witty every day than to say pretty things from time to time."*

— Honoré de Balzac

CHAPTER 28

# Nobody Can Teach Anybody How to Write Dialogue

*"Writers talk too much."*

— Lillian Hellman

I can tell you how to make it funnier, shorter, edgier, longer, tougher, deeper, scarier, smarter, hipper, less formal, and more conversational. But I can't teach you which words the characters should say.

I can assign you a dozen writing exercises in which I give you a dramatic situation, tell you who the characters are, and what the objective of the exercise is... but I can't teach you which words to use.

I can have a course entitled "Writing the Romantic Comedy" in which the goal is to write The Next Great Rom/Com, but I can't teach you how to write clever man/woman banter.

I can show you how to create fully realized, three-dimensional, recognizable human beings with shadings, contours, conflicts, and clear motivations that dictate what they will say and do, but I can't teach you the words that should come out of their mouths.

That's between you and your muse and if your muse isn't available, you're on your own.

# Strategy

## Circumstances Can Get to the Best of Us

At your wit's end. At the end of your rope. Backed into a corner. "I'm as mad as hell and I'm not going to take this anymore."[†] When mean, rotten, bad, terrible people do horrible things it's expected. But when a decent man breaks the laws of God and man and finds himself in circumstances where he must go against everything he believes in, the potential for drama is ripe.

# Writing Exercise

Imagine the person you dislike most is tied up in a chair and you can say anything you want to him/her. Write a one-page, single-spaced monologue venting all of your anger at the person. If you get into it, make it longer. Doing this will stretch your ability to write powerful emotional scenes.

[†] To see the famous scene that made this line a classic, watch *Network* (1976) for Peter Finch's Oscar-winning performance as an enraged TV anchorman.

CHAPTER 29

# Character Motivation Is a Bitch!

*"We write to taste life twice, in the moment and in retrospection."*

— Anaïs Nin

As Shakespeare said, "strong reasons make strong actions." The reason this is so profound is that if you don't know why a character — especially your protagonist — is behaving in a certain way or is in search of something, you will have a rambling screenplay.

Your plot will be unclear and your dialogue, no matter how witty, will mean little once your audience starts wondering why your main character is saying these things.

A long-standing rule of writing: Every line of dialogue should reveal character, move the story forward, or get a laugh. If your line doesn't do any of those things, you need to rethink it.

And it's not just one plot-point in the script. You need to justify every line in every scene. If your protagonist goes into a dry cleaners' shop, she better have a reason. If it's just for her to pick up eleven dresses so we can see that she has excellent taste in clothes, that's not enough of a reason for the scene (unless her taste in fashion is key to the character and plot). We can learn that by looking into her closet.

If she exchanges dialogue with the proprietor who's describing how he removed some difficult stains, that's not reason enough for the dialogue — unless it's a thriller and the proprietor's discussion triggers a memory of hers that will move the plot forward.

If you have her go into that dry cleaners', it must be for a reason germane to the plot or her persona.

I have a friend whose mother is Super Grandma. He has four kids under twelve. When he was growing up he didn't have a grandmother because his mother's mom died early. So my friend and his two sisters grew up without a grandmother.

When my friend and his wife began having children, along with his two sisters and their spouses, his mother very quickly became the greatest grandmother in the world.

I've known this woman all my life. I asked her about being Super Grandma and she said that because her kids had to grow up without a grandmother, she wasn't going to let that happen to *her* grandchildren.

How's that for a strong reason resulting in a strong action?

Whenever I have trouble pinpointing why a character is doing something, I think of her. And it helps me concentrate on giving a character proper motivation.

It's the same with strong personal beliefs. I believe in UFOs. I've read every book on the controversial "alien crash" in 1947 at Roswell, New Mexico, pro and con. I've pored over many UFO websites. The more I absorb, the stronger I believe that we are being visited by extraterrestrials. I have a friend who thinks I'm nuts, or at least naive, or just badly misguided in my search for truth.

We've been disagreeing and arguing about UFOs for years. Whenever I toss out new information, he has something to throw back at me. Our discussions are never heated, but they are passionate. As strongly as I believe in UFOs, he disbelieves. This kind of dialogue results in low-level conflict.

No one will get angry, tempers won't flare, dams of pent-up emotions won't burst. It's just fun, mildly interesting banter.

But if you had a fanatical pro-choice advocate and an equally fanatical pro-life supporter in the same room talking about abortion, you can imagine the heated exchanges that would erupt. This dialogue wouldn't qualify as banter. It's more divisive. More personal. It gets into one's core belief system.

This is serious conflict. But not serious enough for the parties to come to blows, or worse. This is the kind of dialogue and conflict that usually starts off with great civility and winds up with the gloves being taken off; but nobody comes out swinging hard enough to draw blood.

Blood gets drawn (and I mean this symbolically) from visceral situations. A husband confronts his wife's lover. A father confronts his daughter's rapist. A woman confronts the man who killed her son in a drunk-driving accident as he comes out of a bar drunk. These encounters represent conflict in the extreme. No one can know how long they will last or how they will end. These are situations that often result in crimes of passion.

You don't intend to strangle the idiot whose carelessness turned your child into a paraplegic, but angry words lead to unguarded conversation that leads to loss of control and either assault and battery, attempted murder, or murder charges being filed.

Conflict is the soul of dialogue.

Two lovers kissing and cooing are boring, but if they start screaming at each other in public they become riveting. The nature of what you're writing dictates the level and passion of the conflict. This level is dictated by the personalities involved. Two low-key, reasonable people won't react to the same situation as will two high-strung, hot-tempered men with too much testosterone.

But it's more dramatic when the person you least expect to lose it or get violent does so. Likewise, the most appealing drama comes when paradox and irony enter a situation. The white racist male who falls in love with a black woman. The teetotaling moralist arch-conservative who falls for a stripper.

My mild disagreement with my friend is another good example. If I, a true believer in UFOs, see one, it's not dramatic. If he sees one, it is. If I stumble onto secret government files that emphatically prove that every UFO sighting was a hoax, it's dramatic. If my friend stumbled on them, all he'd be doing is saying, "I told you so."

The beauty of conflict is that it helps you figure out what characters will and won't say or *do* in a situation.

A good exercise to see how you handle conflict is writing a five-page scene in which two people who hate each other are stuck in an elevator. Another excellent exercise is to put yourself in that same elevator with the person you hate the most in the world. Five pages. Don't censor the dialogue. You'll be surprised at what you find yourself saying.

# Strategy

## Shakespeare Never Murdered Anybody

Neither did Quentin Tarantino, Raymond Chandler, Joe Eszterhas, David Mamet, William Goldman, the Coen brothers, Shane Black, Robert Rodriguez, Robert Towne, Billy Wilder, the Wachowski brothers, Michael Mann, and hundreds of other screenwriters who wrote nifty scripts in which the main character killed somebody.

So just because you've never murdered anybody doesn't mean you can't write a story about someone who does. And it doesn't mean you can't inhabit the mind of a killer, even if you're a genuinely nice person who doesn't think bad thoughts or revel in the agony of others or curse or swear or have a low opinion of the human race. If you like to think the best of people, don't let your inherent goodness prevent you from creating a mesmerizing killer/kidnapper/traitor/terrorist or all-around rotten person as your main character.

# Writing Exercise

Two people who hate each other inadvertently bump into each other in an elevator. They snub or glare at each other, then the elevator suddenly stops and they're stuck. What do they talk about? Write two different scenes, one from the point of view of each character.

To make it even more interesting, have the elevator stuck in a burning building. There's only enough air for one person to breathe. How determined is each man to be the survivor?

CHAPTER 30

# Never Discuss Religion or Politics. *NOT!*

*"Never say more than is necessary."*

— Richard Brinsley Sheridan

Make sure your characters are at odds, disagreeing, irritating each other, and getting on each other's nerves.

Let them be at variance over little things, big things, small points, huge issues.

Just as in life it's fun to push someone's buttons, it's crucial that this happens in your screenplay. If you want to show a couple in conflict, have them fight over where to eat dinner. The woman wants Chinese, the man wants Mexican. We'll learn volumes about their relationship from this discussion, largely because it won't only be about where they're going to eat.

Talk of a restaurant will invariably lead to one bringing up the other's selfishness, which will lead to one's inflexibility, which will lead to how one is immature, and this will move on to their mutual dislike of each other's friends and in-laws.

As an exercise, write a ten-page scene in which a couple married for seven years argue about where to eat dinner. It can be funny or serious, probably both. You would never have a ten-page scene in your screenplay, but by writing ten pages you'll create intriguing character traits which you would then edit to make it fit.

On the other hand, you *could* use the entire ten-page scene providing you break it up. Two people talking for ten pages in their living room is a lot for a camera to handle. But if it starts in the bedroom, moves to the living room, then goes to their driveway and winds up in their car, it's no longer a ten-page scene but four separate scenes.

# Strategy

## A Last Word on Dialogue

Make sure your characters don't sound alike. Don't have four funny men who hang out together, have *one* funny man. And have another one be humorless. And another one insecure about his intelligence and the last angry at himself for hanging with these losers. A character is confident or shy. Type A or Type B. Life-of-the-party or wallflower. A womanizer or pathologically shy. The more distinctive they sound, the easier it is for you to write dialogue for them.

# PART 4
# FINDING YOUR NICHE

■ ■ ■

*"Consider well what your strength is equal to, and what exceeds your ability."*

— Horace

CHAPTER 31

# Which Is the Right Genre for You?

*"There is nothing new except what is forgotten."*

— Attributed to Mlle. Bertin, milliner to Marie Antoinette

Write whatever you think you can. The problem is deciding what you're best at. If you want to write earnest dramas, but all your story ideas sound like nutty comedies and all your serious dialogue is hilarious, you may want to reconsider. I've read plays by writers who wanted to be the next Ibsen, but discovered that they were really the next Neil Simon (not that that's a bad thing).

On the other hand, I've read screenplays by people who set out to write lighthearted romances, but discovered along the way that their plots were deeper and darker than they first imagined.

I believe that most screenwriters are capable of writing any genre of movie. People pigeonholed as comedy writers could write a heartfelt drama and the rough-and-tumble-action writer could churn out a nutty romantic comedy. I've seen numerous adventure films that were hilarious, just as I've seen comedies with moments that were as serious and profound as the play *Death of a Salesman*... which, by the way, has lots of laughs.

The point is, I think screenwriters should attempt to write for different genres. First of all, it'll be a challenge. Secondly, if you've been writing thrillers and action/adventures with lots of killing, it might be nice to write a small, gentle story, something that might be considered more independent than mainstream.

If you discover that you can write comfortably in a variety of genres, all the better. If you can't handle something different, at least you'll know not to venture too far from the well. This is not to say that every writer can handle every genre ably. The fact is, a few screenwriters can do it all, and the truth is, some writers are better at one genre than another.

Finding the thing you do best is the hard part. There are basically three types of screenplays. Mainstream Hollywood, independent, and made-for-television (films that might be too risky to be released theatrically, but would find an audience on the tube: HBO, Showtime, Hallmark, etc.). But the types of stories are endless.

What follows is a listing of genres and examples of each. To present a framework of reference I've listed three movies for each category.

**Action:** *Salt, Wanted* (2008), *Eagle Eye*

**Action Comedy:** *Iron Man, Mr. and Mrs. Smith* (2005), *Lethal Weapon* series

**Action Thriller:** *Taken, Die Hard, Speed*

**Bio-Pic:** *Julie and Julia, The Blind Side, Hoffa*

**Boys with Toys:** *Transformers, Armageddon, Con Air*

**Chick Flix:** *Sex and the City, He's Just Not That Into You, Legally Blonde*

**Comedy Drama:** *Funny People, As Good as It Gets, The Graduate*

**Coming of Age:** *Stand by Me, An Education, American Graffiti*

**Courtroom Drama:** *Presumed Innocent, The Verdict, Witness for the Prosecution*

**Crime Drama:** *The Godfather I & II, Carlito's Way, Donny Brasco*

**Dark Comedy:** *Happiness, Welcome to the Dollhouse, Eating Raoul*

**Disaster Drama:** *2012, Twister, The Day After Tomorrow*

**Drama:** *Slumdog Millionaire, Precious, Wall Street I & II*

**Earnest Drama:** *Gran Torino, Deep End of the Ocean, Mr. Smith Goes to Washington*

**Family/Children's Comedy:** *Happy Feet, Shrek, Babe*

**Gangster Comedy/Drama:** *Pulp Fiction, Analyze This!, Suicide Kings*

**Historical Drama:** *Gangs of New York, Pearl Harbor* (2002), *Braveheart*

**Horror:** *Paranormal Activity,* Pet Sematary, *The Orphanage*

**Independent Drama:** *Sunshine Cleaning, Little Children, Big Fan*

**Medical Drama:** *A Beautiful Mind, Philadelphia, Lorenzo's Oil*

**Medical Thriller:** *Splice, Outbreak, Coma*

**Mystery:** *Misery, Quarantine, Frenzy*

**Parody:** *Naked Gun* series, *Scary Movie I & II, Hot Shots*

**Period Drama:** *The Age of Innocence, Sense and Sensibility, Gone with the Wind*

**Political Drama/Comedy:** *Wag the Dog, Bulworth, The Candidate*

**Political Thriller:** *Blood Diamond, Parallax View, The Manchurian Candidate* (1962)

**Psychological Thriller:** *Seven, The Silence of the Lambs, Fight Club*

**Romantic Comedy:** *When in Rome, The Proposal, It's Complicated*

**Romantic Drama:** *Vanity Fair, The Unbearable Lightness of Being, The Apartment*

**Sci-Fi Action:** *Children of Men, Cloverfield, Déjà Vu*

**Screwball Comedy:** *Meet the Parents, Some Like It Hot, A Fish Called Wanda*

**Sex Comedy:** *Knocked Up, The 40-Year-Old Virgin, Shampoo,* early Woody Allen

**Slasher/Dead Teenager:** *Scream, I Know What You Did Last Summer, Cabin Fever*

**Sports Drama:** *Breaking Away, Bull Durham, The Karate Kid*

**Suspense Drama:** *Law Abiding Citizen; A Perfect Murder; Sorry, Wrong Number*

**Suspense Thriller:** *The Secret In Their Eyes, Tell No One, I've Loved You So Long*

**War:** *Apocalypse Now, Platoon, Saving Private Ryan*

**Western:** *Butch Cassidy and the Sundance Kid, High Noon, Unforgiven*

**Zany Comedy:** *There's Something About Mary, Dumb and Dumber, A Night at the Opera*

There are many more. And some of the above might easily be cross-genre. Variations on a variation of a variation. Whatever niche your screenplay falls into, it's important to know the kind of screenplay you're writing, especially when you've finished it and need to describe it to someone.

The day will come when you're ready to send it out into the world and someone will ask you what your screenplay is about. Frankly, before that day comes, you'll find yourself at a party or in a bar or at a lecture when you casually mention that you're writing (or you've completed) a screenplay. Trust me: Someone will definitely ask you what it's about. You will sound like a pro if you can rattle off the main storyline in a long sentence or two, pinpoint the genre, and provide the name of an actor — preferably a star — or a hot, up-and-coming actor who would be perfect for the lead.

Get used to this kind of exchange:

> REGULAR PERSON
> You're writing a screenplay? Really?

> YOU
> Yes.

> REGULAR PERSON
> What's it about?

> YOU
> It's a coming-of-age comedy called
> *Sister Sally and Father Nick*. It's
> about a fifteen-year-old girl who
> discovers that her mother is an ex-nun
> and her father is an ex-priest.

Get comfortable hearing yourself talk about what you've written. The day will come — hopefully, many days will come — when you have the opportunity to pitch your ideas to people in the industry. The more comfortable you are talking about the story you've written, the better your pitch will be.

Some screenwriters feel comfortable and natural sitting across from strangers or people they barely know; joking, kidding, schmoozing, and being, in essence, salesmen of their own work. But most of the screenwriters I know aren't very good at it. Understand that it's a skill that can be practiced and improved, so do it every chance you get.

# Writing Exercise

Write a three-paragraph pitch of the last screenplay you wrote or the one you're writing now. Rehearse it, then ask someone close to you to pretend they're a producer, then pitch it to them. Pay attention to how you stumble or stutter or hesitate. You'll be surprised how difficult it is. Practice doing it and you'll get better each time.

# Strategy

## Don't Rule Out Making Your Own Movie

A screenplay is your calling card. If you don't sell it, maybe it'll get you representation, or a producer will read it and like the writing, or the creative spin you put on the dialogue will get you hired for something else. It's all about a way in the door.

Another way in is to make your own film. If you've written a summer blockbuster with tons of special effects, forget about it. But if you've written a script with a small cast, small location, and you have some discretionary money (or have access to it), why not do it yourself?

You'll direct it. You'll find actors. If you're near New York or Los Angeles you'll have lots to choose from. If you're in the hinterlands there are plenty of community theaters from which to draw talent. Maybe you'll cast people you know or family members. Whatever.

The bottom line is that with the cheap digital cameras available today, why not take a chance and make your own movie? (Check out my book *The Portable Film School* for some pointers on shooting a film.)

Remember *the* big movie in 2009? *Paranormal Activity*, written and directed by Oren Peli. Costing approximately $15,000 to make, most of it was shot entirely in Peli's home. There were five people in the cast, two of the parts big roles.

He sold the film rights for $350,000 (meaning a profit of $335,000) and that was just the beginning. He was hired to write and direct another film called *Area 51* and there's a *Paranormal Activity 2* sequel and undoubtedly another and another.

His calling card broke down the gates and launched his career. This might be a way for you, too.

CHAPTER 32

# Is Animation the Way to Go?

*"Animation is about creating the illusion of life.*
*And you can't create it if you don't have one."*

— Brad Bird

First of all, the rules of screenwriting apply equally to an animated film. Just because you're writing about cute animals or people who are drawn, you still need a story. You need characters that have problems. You'll need funny dialogue and subplots and Act II complications and your script will be just as long as a live-action script.

I bring this up because I find that a surprisingly high number of screenwriters wrongly assume that animated screenplays are shorter or should look different.

They don't. They should look just like a normal screenplay.

Deciding to write an animated script is a major career decision, primarily because it's an insular business. It's like an exclusive club that doesn't need any more members.

By that I mean that Pixar, Disney, DreamWorks, and others generate ideas from within. They are reluctant to read spec scripts when they have creative teams who are delivering the goods, i.e., animated films that make big bucks (some more than others, but profitable nevertheless).

Does that mean you shouldn't write your animated script about the family of cute buzzards, loveable snakes, and goofball Gila monsters living in the Mojave Desert whose happy lives are being threatened by an oil refinery?

Of course not. Go for it. But be aware that it could be an even tougher climb up that mountain leading to representation or a deal.

My intention is not to be negative, but realistic. It's harder to break in with a great animated spec. Agents and managers are reluctant to run with a script when they know that they'll be facing a closed shop. So why bother?

My advice is to write a "normal" screenplay. Work hard to get representation, then hope for a deal, then pray that it gets made and that it makes some noise.

Once that's happened, you'll be in a different position. You'll be a screenwriter who's had a movie made and if it's a hit, you'll be a screenwriter with a hit under your belt.

You'll be looked at differently and you'll have access to people who actually want to meet you.

That's when you pitch your animated script (or pull it out and hand it to them if you've written it). At this point you'll be swimming in different waters and you and your script will have a much better chance.

# Writing Exercise

Come up with three ideas for an animated screenplay with an animal as the main character of one, a child the main character of another, and a vampire the main character of the third. Remember, the characters in animated films have the same problems that human beings have and they must have something important that they want.

# Strategy

## The Best Coming-of-Age Stories Are
## Written by People Who've Come of Age

I've been paying close attention to the Academy Awards all my life. I've checked the ages of the winners of the two screenwriting categories: Best Original Screenplay and Best Screenplay from Another Source. The winners under thirty have been damn few. And the winners under twenty-five are zero. Most Oscar-winning screenwriters are well into their thirties and up. I wonder why? Is it because, maybe just maybe, they've learned a few things about life and the human condition and they've been able to translate that knowledge into intelligent scripts? Young screenwriters just don't have enough in them to deliver the goods.

Except, of course, in 1998. *Good Will Hunting* was written by Matt Damon and Ben Affleck, who were both in their mid-twenties. Adding to the fairy tale aspect of their success (they were struggling actors and wrote the script for themselves) they received more than $500,000 for their screenplay. Good for them. Even after the 50-50 split, taxes, and agent commissions, we're talking nice money.

But when I first heard of their good fortune, my immediate reaction was this: If they were two actors in their forties who'd been struggling since their first scene study course at the American Academy of Dramatic Arts twenty years ago, not only would the script probably not have been made or sold, but the perception would've been that these were two middle-aged losers.

Their age wouldn't have had the sheen of the two young guys and I don't think they could have gotten it read, let alone made, let alone being allowed to star in it. There's enough prejudice toward new writers: It's even worse for *older* new writers.

I have nothing but the best wishes for any writer of any age. However, Hollywood's preoccupation with youth is a fact that all screenwriters must deal with. Despite whatever ageism exists in Hollywood, it doesn't mean you shouldn't try. If a screenplay lands on an agent's or producer's desk and she loves it, she won't suddenly dismiss it when she finds out the author has thinning gray hair, just started menopause, or has two grandchildren. Your script is everything.

So if you're closer to forty than thirty, reinvent yourself. You've loved movies all your life. Take a shot at writing one: Make a dent in the system and prove Hollywood wrong.

CHAPTER 33

# You're Over 30 and Starting Your First Script. What Do You Do?

*"A talent is formed in stillness,*
*a character in the world's torrent."*

— Johann Wolfgang von Goethe

There's an old maxim: It's about what's between the pages, not about the age of the person who wrote them.

If you're over thirty, you'll never be called the hot *young* screenwriter. Or the gifted *kid* fresh out of UCLA's Screenwriting Program. Or the *girl* wonder who churned out a tearjerker spec script while working weekends at Blockbuster. Or the geeky *teenaged* movie nut still on his parents medical benefits plan who wrote the edgy, teen-angst thriller that went for $450,000 in a fierce studio bidding war.

The notion that early success is somehow sweeter is nice to ponder, but the fact is most screenwriters don't make it when they're young, i.e., let's say under thirty. There are exceptions, of course. But from my experience, the best writing comes from older writers, i.e., thirty and upward. Some of these "older writers" may have been toiling away since they were in college or their early twenties, but their success came after some dues paying.

*This* is the mistake Hollywood has been making.

It all comes down to what's on the page, not the age of the person who wrote what's there.

The reason I define older screenwriters as thirty and beyond is because most have had other careers — perhaps successful careers, but they've reached that point in life where they want to go after a dream they've always had: They want to write a movie.

Some of the careers of my older students include the following:

actors • art dealer • computer programmers • copywriters • CPA • doctors • graphic designers • high school English teacher • insurance agents (life. health, disability) • lawyers (criminal, civil) • mafioso's wife • mother of triplets • multi-millionaire corporate exec • musical chorale director • psychiatrists (Freudian, Gestalt) • secretaries • speechwriter • TV producers • voice-over performer

If you're no longer in your twenties, you need to look at the advantages that come with not being "young."

experience • mileage • hindsight • insight • patience • introspection • retrospection • frames of reference • loss • travel • disillusion • personal evolution • therapy • a twelve-step program

But there are disadvantages, too. It's a lot easier to put up with bullshit at twenty-three than at thirty-seven. Younger people have a higher tolerance for it.

Like being in a meeting with someone who falls asleep while you talk to her. If that happened in your present business life, you'd be insulted and probably leave the room or point out how rude the person was.

But if it were an upper echelon producer (or even a bottom-feeder who makes only straight-to-video schlock) who dozed off during a crucial pitch meeting, you'd have to ignore it, grit your teeth, and keep on talking.

Could you do that? Could you swallow the comfortable pride you've developed? Could you put that self-esteem you've worked so hard to attain on the line?

That scenario actually happened to me during a get-acquainted meeting with a producer well into her seventies. She began the session with wide-eyed enthusiasm, but several minutes into it, I noticed that her eyes had closed and she had nodded off.

There were several people in the room during this meeting, so after recovering from the shock of this sleeping woman, without missing a beat I turned to her two assistants and continued my pitch pretending, as they did, that she wasn't asleep.

While the same experience can happen to young writers and be just as demeaning for them, this kind of gauche behavior is more difficult to take for the "older" writer, new or otherwise. You're just not used to having your dignity assaulted without reacting.

Successful salesmen know that making the sale is the ultimate goal. They put up with all their clients' nonsense, irrational demands, and conflicting directions to get the sale (or until they've had enough and walk away). Screenwriters must have the same philosophy. Unfortunately, it's easier to put up with someone's crap when you're young and hungry.

When you're older you need help. If you're a man over forty, what would you give for good knees and serious erections? This is where humility, maturity, patience, and savvy enter the picture. If you want the deal, bite the bullet. And if a producer or development executive veers off into humiliation and degradation, bite harder or, like the sales-man who has had enough, walk away.

Either way, though your pride may have been bruised, it will make for a good anecdote. Just like most of the other hurtful/terrible/sad/nasty/dangerous/heartbreaking things that happen to us.

Are you getting the picture?

All the crap you've gone through combined with the joyful high points of your life are worth something to you as a screenwriter and storyteller.

# Strategy

## Make Points on the Last Page of Your Script

I call them "ending endings." Your screenplay has answered the major dramatic question. Let's say it is, "Will boy over-come all obstacles and get girl?" Your ending's a happy one. He gets her. Most of the time all you need is a Fade Out and you're done.

Other times, depending upon the genre, you can make an ending more satisfying by including an "ending" ending: Think of it as a subtle grace note that lends irony or expectation.

# Viewing Exercise

For some superb films with "ending endings," check out the following: *The Usual Suspects*, *Silence of the Lambs*, *Body Heat*, *Planet of the Apes* (1968), and *Fight Club*.

From *The Godfather*...
"Moe Greene was a great man....
Someone put a bullet through his
eye. No one knows who gave the
order. When I heard it, I wasn't angry; I knew Moe. I knew he was
headstrong, talking loud, saying
stupid things. So when he turned
up dead, I let it go. And I said to
myself, this is the business we've
chosen. I didn't ask who gave the
order, because it had nothing to do
with business!"

Hyman Roth to Michael Corleone

■  ■  ■

*"Luck never gives; it only lends."*
                    — Swedish proverb

CHAPTER 34

# Game Plan No. 1
# Sing One Song,
# But Sing it Well

Once you've found your ideal genre, you might find it's all you can do. Actually, it may be the only thing a studio or network might *allow* you to do. You will be pigeon-holed. Although this may seem extreme, it's not as bad as it sounds. Let's say you break in with a caper script. It gets some good buzz and it's a huge hit. You'll be bombarded with offers to rewrite other caper scripts or with ideas from producers for caper scripts that are barely vague premises. But because you wrote that caper script that became a big hit, you're the caper guy.

If you get a second caper movie deal and it too is a success, you'll still be viewed as the caper guy, but you might get a little clout. This will mean more offers to rewrite or polish more caper scripts and you might do a couple just for the bucks or to make points with a big time producer and that won't be so bad either.

Ultimately, if you're lucky and you're viewed as someone who can deliver good caper scripts and good caper-script rewrites, you might be able to parlay that into a deal where you actually get to write a script that isn't a caper, or someone will produce your drama-with-the-Indie-feel about a sensitive poet in Missouri who nurses a coyote back to health and finds true love with the local vet that you wrote six years ago.

But before that can happen, you need to pay your dues doing what you're perceived as doing best: caper movies. In the peculiar wisdom of Hollywood, you'll be the writer who knows only one song, but you can sing it well.

So do what you are asked until you learn another song.

CHAPTER 35

# Game Plan No. 2 Don't Become a Cautionary Tale

Screenwriters without an agent or manager have no choice but to try to make things happen themselves. If you don't know anyone, you must get to know people. To accomplish this you need to be thick-skinned and have a little luck on your side.

Until a few years ago, a screenwriter without connections could at least send a query letter with a self-addressed stamped envelope and get some kind of response. But now many of the bigger agencies won't even read those. They'll send them back unread. And with spam-blockers it's pretty much impossible to get an email through to someone.

So what does an unrepresented screenwriter have to do to get his work read?

There's no easy answer, other than to learn how to be unafraid to ask everyone you know who may be somehow connected to someone who is in "the business" for help. This isn't easy to do. If you are particularly well-mannered or shy, it will be extremely difficult. If you are brazen and don't care what people think and have the "I won't take no for an answer" salesman bravura, it will be easier… and I use the term *easier* with big quotes. *Big* quotes.

Until an agent or manager signs you as a client, moving your career forward is up to you. And that means doing whatever it takes to get your script into the hands of someone who can move it to the next level. The harder you work at meeting people who can help you, the better your odds of making that big sale. But even then, there are no guarantees.

To wit (this is a true story)...

A screenwriter friend had finished a screenplay. A comedy. I read it and thought it to be quite good, funny, and commercial. He had a handful of people he could ask for help in getting representation. The first person he called came through for him in spades. He couldn't help him find an agent, but he had access to a major Hollywood player.

This individual, himself a producer, had become friends with the sister and brother-in-law of a big time Hollywood director. Actually, the director was more than big time. Let's just say he is upper echelon.

So when the screenwriter hears the name of the director, his hopes soar. Then, those hopes soar even higher when he is told by the producer to drop off his screenplay to the office of the director's brother-in-law.

Residing near the brother-in-law's office (and to save on the postage), the screenwriter decides to drop off the manuscript in person. He goes to the office, knocks on the door, and a receptionist greets him. He holds up the envelope containing his screenplay and asks if she can get this to so-and-so. His sole intent is to just leave it with the receptionist.

But she misinterprets what the screenwriter says, asks for his name, picks up the phone, calls the brother-in-law and says that there's someone here to see him. The screenwriter doesn't say he just wanted to leave the script.

A secretary comes out, and before the screenwriter can say a word, says "Mr. So-and-So will be with you in a few minutes. Come with me."

The screenwriter follows her into a small meeting room where he is told to wait. After a few minutes, the brother-in-law arrives. Again, the screenwriter is prepared to simply introduce himself, hand over the screenplay, thank the man for getting it to his famous brother-in-law, and then leave.

But the brother-in-law, a very nice man, wants to talk. So they talk. For more than an hour. About movies and stars and the big time director. The screenwriter feels comfortable with the brother-in-law and the conversation goes so well that the subject of getting together for lunch in the future is brought up.

So far, so good. Now for the bad news. The brother-in-law proceeds to explain that he will not be giving the screenplay to the big time director to read, but instead to the big time director's sister.

Yes. Sister.

This stuns the screenwriter. The brother-in-law proceeds to explain that his wife reads scripts for her high-profile director brother — scripts that come to her via people she meets in her business, which (now this is important) is *not* show business. The sister is in a field that is far removed from Hollywood and it literally has nothing whatsoever to do with the ability to read and judge the merits of a screenplay.

The horrible truth is all beginning to fall into place for the screenwriter. If the director's sister likes the screenplay, she will pass it on to him. But what the screenwriter starts to wonder is whether or not the director will actually give any credence to his sister's opinion of a screenplay.

Why should he? The director is so prominent that he has his own production company receiving scripts from the best agents and managers representing the best screenwriters... so why would he give a damn what his sister — who's not even in show business — thinks about a script? He wonders, like, "duh!"

Despite his misgivings, the screenwriter gives his screenplay to the brother-in-law, they shake hands and part in a friendly "We'll get together soon" manner with the brother-in-law saying, "My wife will get back to you after she reads the screenplay."

The screenwriter smiles and leaves. The instant he walks out of the office his heart sinks. His gut instinct is that nothing will come of this. He goes home and googles the name of the director's sister-in-law and, as he suspected, finds not one mention of her film credits or anything to do with show business or Hollywood. He does, however, find several hits concerning the business that she *is* in. And he can't help but wonder if the reason she is successful in her field is because of her connection to her famous brother. He doesn't know. He can't be sure. But it's not all that far-fetched. He's starting to over-analyze the situation.

Despite his misgivings, he decides to put a happy face on the experience. He started to imagine that the director's sister will love the script and pass it on to her brother and that he will like it and a phone call will be made and a meeting and a six-figure deal and the house in Malibu and....

Five months passed. No contact. The screenwriter's happy face scenario turned into a sad face, but not a defeated face because screenwriters cannot allow themselves to be defeated. That would mean giving up. And that particular screenwriter doesn't have it in his genetic makeup to quit. He's a big believer in living and learning, being cautiously optimistic, and having a healthy cynicism about these things.

The only downside is that now, whenever the screenwriter sees or hears the name of the famous director and news of his various upcoming projects, the screenwriter can't help but wonder if the director's sister was responsible for finding any of the scripts. After a few seconds, he laughs at the thought of it. But most importantly, this screenwriter has had a valuable experience that he can draw upon the next time he has the chance to meet someone who might help further his career. His emotions will be a mix of cautious optimism and healthy cynicism, but he'll go in with eyes wide open, a lot wiser.

CHAPTER 36

# Game Plan No. 3 Never Underestimate the Persuasiveness of a Producer

No matter how smart or shrewd you may be, no matter what your education or ability to handle willful people is, no matter how strong your resolve and sense of righteousness, be warned: Not all producers are nice.

I once did script-consulting for a sixty-eight-year-old retired loan shark who was writing a screenplay about his early years as a bookie. They didn't come any tougher than this guy. He did time in prison. He had dealings with the mob. After he finished his screenplay, which was quite good, he had an element of bravado and confidence that he would sell his script fast. He was counting the money. I cautioned him, saying that if he thought it was tough dealing with the mob, wait until he got a taste of the Hollywood system. He thought I was kidding. Within three months he was calling me, shaking his head in confusion because he'd had his first dealing with a movie producer. "You were right," he said. "You were right."

■ ■ ■

There are two kinds of producers new screenwriters meet: those who are Writers Guild of America signatories and those who aren't. A signatory company is one that has signed a collective bargaining agreement with WGA. Guild members are prohibited from working for or selling their work to non-signatory companies.

Once you've sold a screenplay or TV script to a signatory, you must join the Writers Guild, which is a good thing because you get benefits, a pension plan, and someone to keep track of your royalties and make sure you get paid. From that point on in your career you cannot work for a non-signatory.

However, until you've sold that first script, working for non-signatories is legal, ethical, and a way to build up a credit or two. The problem is that you will get less money than the minimums stipulated by the Writers Guild or no money at all. This isn't such a bad deal. I've known dozens of screenwriters, especially those who wanted to direct, who broke into the business this way.

If there's a negative to going this route it's because of the producer. You may be wondering why producers and/or production companies don't automatically become official Writers Guild signatories. The reason is... (take a guess)... money. They may have a tiny budget or a larger budget that they'd rather use for actor's salaries or production values. Their logic is to get a new screenwriter to work for peanuts and use the money that would normally go to you to have a good-looking wig made for the lead character.

If you look at it from a producer's point of view, it makes sense. Instead of paying you the Writers Guild minimum, he'll pay you two thousand bucks (or less) to write a screenplay from an idea of his. The downside is that he may ask you to do a million drafts. Okay. Kidding. But he'll ask you for a lot. What's a lot? How does fifteen sound? I know someone who did fifty-five drafts. But the movie got made, which made all the angst worthwhile.

Another downside is that he may want his girlfriend or wife (or both) to be in the film, playing a key part, most likely the lead. Even though she's wrong for the part: can't act, too old, can't remember her lines, changes her lines, fights with the director. Did I say can't act?

The thing is, this movie will in all probability get made because the producer has his financing in order. How he got it you don't know and he won't tell you, but it's probably from wheeling and dealing and lying and sweet-talking and... you get the idea. He may also have lined up distribution rights. What's that? One of the most crucial parts of *any* film deal. Simply, if a producer has made a film, the goal is to get it seen by the public. To make this happen he needs to find a company that distributes films to theaters. In exchange for the right to distribute a film, these companies will commit to getting the finished film into theaters. If a producer can't get a distribution deal, he's basically screwed.

So if you're working for someone who's landed distribution, lucky you. If not, two things could happen. The producer distributes it himself, which is a monumental task. He has to cherry-pick where the film will be shown. This usually involves going to Europe and trying to find money there. The words "finding money" are the bane of any producer's existence.

If he can't find enough money or get a distributor, the movie will go straight to DVD. Don't despair. Even that's not so bad. So you'll have a DVD you can tell your friends to buy or rent, and more importantly, you'll have a credit.

What follows are examples of the behavior of two producers. Let's call them Peter and Paul.

## PETER

*"Hollywood money isn't money. It's congealed snow, melts in your hand, and there you are."*

— Dorothy Parker

Paul had read a screenplay of mine and liked it. Not enough to option it or try to get a studio to buy it, but enough to call me in for a meeting to talk about doing a rewrite of another script he had optioned. I didn't know it at the time, but he was not a Writers Guild signatory. It never occurred to me to ask because he had produced seven films, two of which were major features.

I just assumed he was. Remember that old saying you heard when you were in high school where the teacher writes the word ASSUME on the blackboard, then proceeds to deconstruct it like this: ASS U ME

Then he says "Never assume, because you make an *ass* of *you* and *me*."

So I meet with the guy and he tells me about the project and I have a feel for the material and he mentions a major star for the lead. So far, so good. He asks me to read the script. I take it home and read it. It's a good story, but the script was an epic, taking place over thirty-seven years. I felt it needed to be condensed, called the producer, and in a few sentences told him how I'd do it. He loved my suggestions. He said he wanted to hire me. Then he asked me a question:

"Are you in the Writers Guild?"

I responded yes.

"Then we'll have to work around that."

I started to get that sinking feeling. As a Writers Guild member I knew I wasn't allowed to work under a non-guild contract. But I needed the money and the credit so rather than kill the deal I asked him to explain.

He did so by telling me that he would get the money guy, i.e., the person who would be financing the production, to become a signatory. That's what happened. That individual, let's call him Dave, would became a Writers Guild signatory and all money paid to me would come through his company, which made it fine and dandy with the Guild.

But Peter the producer was still calling the shots. Why wouldn't he become a signatory himself? Because he had approximately eleven other projects in the works, all with non–Writers Guild members who were working for him at bargain basement prices or for no money at all. Some of these screenwriters were fresh out of film school or were in their mid-to-late twenties. They knew they were being taken advantage of, but they also knew there was real potential for getting a movie made.

The plus of getting a movie made is that, even if it's not very good, even if it's downright horrible, in the way Hollywood views careers, you're in a better place than a screenwriter who has never had a movie made.

It makes no sense, but that's how it is.

## PAUL

*"Pretend inferiority and encourage his arrogance."*

— Sun Tzu

He was a charming, charismatic, successful man whom women loved and men envied. While dabbling in the movie business, he also produced plays. Over the course of four years he produced two plays I'd written that were done in Los Angeles.

We became friends. I even stayed at his beautiful home in the Hollywood Hills. I had my own room. My bed was turned down each night by a maid. By the time I got out of the shower in the morning my bed had been made. He had a sauna. A hot tub. A pool. His live-in chef prepared breakfast every day. He gave me the use of one of his cars.

We stayed in touch for a few more years. If I wrote a play that I thought he might like, I'd send it to him. None caught his fancy, then he decided to stop producing plays.

Several years passed and we had no contact.

I'm one of those people who remember obscure dates, birthdays in particular. Birthdays of people I don't really know. If I'm at a party and someone I've never met and may never see again mentions when her birthday is, I'll remember it.

So after roughly ten years without any contact, I glanced at my calendar and remembered that it was his birthday. I decided to call him. He was thrilled to hear from me. We spent a few minutes catching up, then I casually said, "It's hard to believe we haven't talked in ten years."

Instead of saying, "Yeah," or "Right," he says, "What are you talking about? We talked last week!"

The rest of the conversation was pretty much me saying we didn't talk last week and him saying we did. I could feel him getting exasperated and he responded as if I were a difficult child. Although he never got angry at me during the two times we worked together, I knew he could be very intimidating if he were crossed. This had been a friendly call that was turning sour. I knew this was a battle I couldn't win so I let it go and after a minute or so of chatter we ended the call.

Here's the weird thing. I *knew* that I hadn't called him. Knew it with all my heart. But he was so persuasive that by the time we hung up, I was starting to wonder if I had indeed called him.

I couldn't let it go. I was filled with such doubt that I checked my phone records.

There was no record of me calling him, which was my proof. That was my home phone. This was before cell phones.

The only other phone I used was at an office I shared with three other people and it wasn't my phone, so checking the records was impossible.

I tried to shake off the idea that I had called him and forgotten, but I tend to hold on to things for a few hours. I assumed by the time I woke up the next morning it would be out of my head.

But it didn't go away.

Periodically, that conversation pops into my brain and I relive the thing all over again.

He's still in my head.

And after all these years, I still have moments of doubt.

CHAPTER 37

# Game Plan No. 4 Never Forget That There Is No Instant Gratification for Screenwriters

Let's say you think of yourself as a results-oriented person. Now you're in the delayed-gratification world of Hollywood.

Screenwriting is not a profession for anyone who's used to being paid after putting in a day's work. Punch in, punch out. Do your forty hours. Get a paycheck at the end of the week. If you went to college, you put in your four years and you got a degree. Put in two or three more years for grad school and you get a degree. Put in however long it takes to write your dissertation and you have a PhD.

You put in the effort and you get a reward. Makes sense. What doesn't make sense is when you put in the effort and there's no reward. Writing a spec screenplay — whether you spend five weeks, eight months, or two years — doesn't guarantee a reward.

For some, that's very upsetting, especially if you're a results-oriented person. Most of us are results-oriented. Who wants to do anything without some remuneration? Even a college student who gets a job as an unpaid intern will have a payback down the road; experience, maybe a promotion to a paying job upon graduation, possibly a good reference. So there is a payback.

But if you take up screenwriting you must accept the fact that your results-oriented work ethic doesn't mean crap. You have entered a new world of delayed gratification. Put in the time — months, years, lots of sweat and energy — with the idea that there will be a payoff later on.

There might be. There might not. No matter how good or commercial your first screenplay is, it may never earn you a penny or get you an agent. Its only purpose may be to have helped you get your feet wet as a screenwriter. Same with your second, third, fourth, and fifth screenplay.

Lots of hard work, but no deals, agents, or managers. Maybe access to a few producers, which is something. But with each script, you're getting better. Most of us, myself included, after we've written a few screenplays, can look objectively at our first or second and realize that they were at best, workmanlike. Maybe even pretty mediocre.

Delayed gratification should be your mantra. "I will do the work and put in the time because I believe in myself and my talent. I understand that this is a marathon and it's not fair and that some people sell the first freakin' thing they write. I can no longer follow my results-oriented attitude and must accept the fact that I hopefully will taste the honey at some point. I know that the more I write the better I'll get, and that has to be consolation enough until my payday comes."

If you can't abide by this way of thinking, screenwriting will be a troubling, frustrating experience.

CHAPTER 38

# Game Plan No. 5
# Don't Be Too Trusting. Assume Everyone Is Lying Until the Check Clears (and Maybe Even Then).

Thomas S. Szasz said, "The stupid neither forget nor forgive; the naïve forgive and forget; the wise forgive but do not forget."

As a script consultant and writing coach, I often give advice, guidance, and occasionally therapy to many of my clients long after their screenplays are finished. If they've had a negative experience with a producer, agent, development person, director, or manager, they call me looking for an explanation and advice.

I'm not talking only about young screenwriters fresh out of film school or kids with a dream from small-town America. I've worked with people in their thirties, forties, fifties, and sixties who've been successful in other fields, but when it comes to making something happen with their finished screenplay, all the life skills they've learned disappear.

Hard-nosed cops and high-priced attorneys are intimidated by twenty-five-year-old development executives.

Type A stockbrokers fall to pieces as their scripts are turned into mishmash by a producer. Psychiatrists, all kinds of doctors, seen-it-all journalists, firefighters, real estate biggies, housewives, and bookies behave like meek twelve-year-olds when their phone calls aren't returned.

Simply put, they are totally ill-equipped to function as businessmen and businesswomen in Hollywood. They have the talent, but not the know-how to make their career happen.

I understand this. I used to be that way when I first started out. Underlying the behavior is a fear that if you're "not nice" or "not cooperative" or that if you "don't know your place," the person you're dealing with (who you're convinced could be the person that gets you in the door) won't like it if you disagree or stand up for your rights.

One of the reasons I can give people advice or talk them through whatever happened is because I'm a screenwriter myself with my own share of horrifying experiences to draw upon.

I've learned to talk the talk and walk the walk, and, as I often joke, lived to tell about it without losing my sense of humor.

Besides writing an excellent script (which is also her calling card), a screenwriter must also become savvy and shrewd, with the demeanor to continue along the rocky road of selling a script and getting it on the screen without losing her dignity.

CHAPTER 39

# Game Plan No. 6
# Finish the
# Effing Script

The ultimate goal of every screenwriter is to sell a script and get it made. However, the *primary* goal of every screenwriter should be to finish the first draft of a screenplay. Screenwriters run out of steam at various points in a script, but it seems that most hit the wall as they approach the end of the second act. Working toward a 110-page draft that's approximately 37 pages away from the end.

Without a first draft you'll be stuck in a place worse than Development Hell. You're left without food or water in a dark, sad, bleak place that I call Undeveloped Hell. And what's even more galling is that you're the Gatekeeper.

Never forget: a bad *first* draft is preferable to a brilliant unfinished 49 pages that have been gnawing away at you for two years.

Completion of the first draft is everything. Even if it's barely 85 pages with a meandering second act, no real plot twists in Act III, and an ending that's not only unsatisfying, but so wrong it belongs in a different screenplay. Even if it's way too long (and you've known it's too long ever since you hit page 118 and you haven't gotten to the end of Act II), you've got something.

But too short or too long, at least you got to the Fade Out and you've typed The End. Only then can the real work of revision, rethinking, and fine-tuning begin. But getting to that completed first draft is the hardest part for most of us. If you can get a handle on why you're not moving forward to completion, it might help you break through the miasma.

There are several roadblocks that bring screenwriters down. Based on an unscientific poll of screenwriters I know, the following seem to be the biggest barriers.

## 10 Major Roadblocks to Writers: An Unscientific Poll

1) You're spreading yourself too thin with your full-time job, social life, family responsibilities, and/or other interests that prevent you from finding enough quality writing time.

2) You're working on too many scripts at once. Halfway done with this one, a third of the way with that, stuck with no third act for another.

3) You're so infatuated (or obsessed) with your idea that it's turning into a creepy little Pygmalion scene or a psychotic Frankenstein monster. You just can't let it go. You're constantly tweaking and revising the same scenes over and over again.

4) You're spending too much time thinking about the deal you're convinced you'll get or making notes about which stars to get the script to.

5) You get mad at the script, as if it's a recalcitrant child who won't listen.

6) You somehow expect the screenplay to fix itself.

7) You're waiting for your muse to do her part and you haven't realized that she's like that girl/guy who dumped you and left town without a forwarding address.

8) You have negative people around you who are discouraging.

9) You're just lazy and more of a slacker than you thought.

10) You've let yourself drift into a frame of mind where you have become so vulnerable and needy that you've lost confidence in your vision.

Whichever point(s) above applies to you, there's only one way to deal with your inability to see a first draft through to the end: confront it.

It's almost like going to therapy. You acknowledge your problem, figure out why you're letting yourself be victimized by it, then take the necessary steps to get out from under it. Owning up to what you're doing wrong (or not doing) is the first step.

Some problems are easier to deal with than others. If your brother or a parent or even a significant other ridicules or minimizes you for pursuing a screenwriting career, you must turn a deaf ear to the negativity. Let them carry on, smile, and keep writing. It's your dream, not theirs.

If you come to the conclusion that your biggest problem is laziness, i.e., you *talk* about writing a screenplay more often than you actually do it, you *must* give yourself a wake-up call. Stop goofing off. Stop wasting time. Instead of going out drinking with your friends, shopping at the mall, and doing all those things you do to avoid sitting at your computer and grinding out five more pages (even if they're so-so), find a mirror, stare long and hard into it, and remind yourself that writing screenplays isn't a day at the beach.

It is hard to write a screenplay. Very hard. And it takes discipline, concentration, and tenacity to finish one.

CHAPTER 40

# Game Plan No. 7
# Be Smart About
# What You Write

Always write the story you want to tell rather than the story you think will be easier to sell. Nothing is easier to sell. You might have a better shot at getting a deal with a romantic comedy or a guy film than a historical drama about The Hundred Years War or a biographical film about Franklin Delano Roosevelt's second vice-president, but it's best to get the word *easier* out of your vocabulary.

The downside of writing the story you want to tell is that it might not have, excuse the cliché, a snowball's chance in hell. Scripts with protagonists in their seventies or eighties (and even sixties) will be tough sells. When people have come to me with love stories or buddy films about septuagenarians, I always caution them: Write it, but odds are you won't get anywhere with it. You might not even get an agent or producer to read it. There are always exceptions, sure, but if you have another idea with a broader range, write that. And if you think I'm being a know-it-all, go ahead, write the "old person" story and prove me wrong. The worst that can happen is you'll have another writing sample under your belt.

Being smart about what you write means being aware of what's going on in Hollywood. Keep current as to what kind of scripts are being bought, and I don't necessarily mean scripts by established screenwriters. There are websites (updated regularly) that list screenplays that have been sold. Also, read the industry papers like *Variety* and *The Hollywood Reporter* to see what's being bought.

Don't write a script that would have been perfect for audiences of the seventies or eighties but is outdated now because of cultural and social change. There are films being made now that wouldn't have stood a chance twenty, thirty, or forty years ago and vice versa.

When you write a script, always have a star or recognizable actor/actress in mind for the lead character(s). Why? So you can tell agents, managers, and producers who might read the screenplay to picture so-and-so in the lead. A good way of saying it is, "Ideal casting would be Jack Black and Will Farrell." Or "Picture Anne Hathaway in the lead and Zac Efron as the romantic subplot." Sometimes it's good to make a list of three or four actors who would be right in the part. It's a minor detail, but when I read a script and envision a specific actor in the part, it adds another dimension.

CHAPTER 41

# Game Plan No. 8 Ten Checkpoints Your Screenplay Must Pass Before It's Ready to Go

1)  Does it get started soon enough?

2)  Is what the main character wants clearly established, do we know why she wants it, do you make it clear *why* she wants it *now*, and what will happen if she doesn't get it?

3)  Are there enough obstacles challenging the main character?

4)  Do we get a sense that the main character has an internal conflict that affects her behavior?

5)  Is the character somebody we can root for, even if she isn't especially likable?

6)  Are there enough twists and turns so that the storyline isn't predictable?

7)  Do we feel emotionally involved with the plight of the main character?

8) Does the line of dramatic tension intensify as the story moves toward the ending?

9) Is there a change, big or small, in the way the main character now behaves?

10) Is there a satisfying ending? Not necessarily happy or dark or sad, but simply satisfying.

CHAPTER 42

# Game Plan No. 9
# Some Bottom-of-the-Ninth, Last-Minute Practical Advice

- Character descriptions. Let the person reading your script know what he's looking at. Don't just say, "Amanda enters." Is she 16 years old, 54, 87? Is she hot, anorexic, or 300 pounds? Try this: AMANDA, 23, enters. Girl next door, athletic, shy. Or RICK, 30, enters. A muscle-bound, arrogant, pretty boy. Do this for all your major characters, but not for incidental roles.

- Give your protagonist and central characters last names.

- Action/stage directions/screen directions (call them what you will), less is more. Pages filled with too many instructions are a pain in the ass to read. Don't turn off a reader by inundating her with too many words. Make your script fun to read, not ponderous.

- Parentheticals. Avoid them unless absolutely necessary. They slow down the reading process. Most actors ignore them anyway.

- Make sure your characters don't sound alike.

- The more characters you have, the more personas you have to create. The more you have to create, the harder it will be to come up with distinct personalities.

- Make sure every character and every scene has a dramatic purpose, even if it's a small one. If a scene (or character) has no dramatic purpose, get rid of it.

- Avoid monologues and long speeches. If you absolutely must have one, put it in Act III rather than on page 4. If I'm emotionally invested in a character, I'll happily read a monologue, but if it occurs too early in the script, it will just be a mass of words to slog through.

- Dialogue should be conversational. Back and forth. Listen to the way people talk in real life.

- If you're writing a comedy, make sure it's funny. Let your reader know it's a comedy from the first page. If you can cram in three funny lines or situations on the first page, great. If you can get the reader laughing by the time she turns to the second page, fabulous. If you can make her laugh on every page, terrific. Just keep her laughing.

- If your intent is to write a nutty, zany comedy in the vein of the Farrelly brothers, make sure it's nutty and zany, not just clever and amusing. Some comedies are witty, some satirical, some irreverent. Whatever kind you're writing, make sure it's funny. Did I say that you should make sure it's funny? Make sure it's funny.

- If you're writing a thriller or mystery, make sure it's exciting and scary.

- If you're writing an action/adventure, make sure there's plenty of — you get the idea.

- Come up with a good title. *The Dying Gaul* (2005), written and directed by Craig Lucas, is a film (about a screenwriter, ironically) adapted from his play of the same name. Terrific play, wonderful film, horrible title. It won't draw in crowds at the cineplexes, nor does it suggest that it would be a good date movie. It doesn't imply fun or adventure or, well, anything. Most people will have to think twice as to what a Gaul is. And the word "dying" is a bummer. A good title might help a bad script get read. A bad title might dissuade a reader from wanting to like it.

- Listen to criticism and feedback, but in the end, accept and reject what your gut tells you. No critic, teacher, or consultant is one hundred percent right. After all the input and revisions, it is you who ultimately must take control of the project.

CHAPTER 43

# Game Plan No. 10
# A Satisfying
# Ending

*"You must write for yourself, above all. That is your only hope of creating something beautiful."*

— Gustave Flaubert

I used to enjoy gambling in casinos. I always went into one filled with the hope that I'd win a chunk of money. On a good night, I'd actually come out ahead and feel great. On most nights I'd lose or break even and I'd be filled with disappointment as I walked out. But even as I left I knew I'd try again the next night, and the hope I had at the start of the evening began to grow once more. By the next evening, the disappointment was forgotten and the hope that I'd win a chunk of money had filled me again.

Pursuing a career as a screenwriter is like that. Hope and disappointment. You hope your script is terrific. You hope each person who reads it loves it. You hope you get an agent. You hope you get a producer and studio interested in your script. You just keep hoping and hoping and hoping. And when nothing has happened on that particular script, you experience disappointment. Then you must resolve to start another script. Once you do so, your hopes will return.

This is how it works. Most screenwriters don't sell their first screenplay. Some do, but that happens so rarely that it's not part of the equation. Most screenwriters serve their apprenticeship and write a handful of scripts before attracting any interest. With each script they're filled with hope. And when each one has been passed on enough, the disappointment returns and these writers start writing their next screenplay to renew their hope.

At the end of the day, being a screenwriter is all about tenacity and patience. You're running in a marathon. How long can you last? Frankly, you can last as long as you choose if you love the creativity and the process of writing screenplays.

As for getting that first sale? Simply, it's about luck, timing, connections, right place at the right time, right concept at the right time, and the gods. And as I mentioned earlier, somebody important has to say it's good. Maybe that person has to love it. Somebody with enough access or clout to champion your script through the corridors of Hollywood or the less-crowded hallways of the world of independent films.

When people find out I teach screenwriting, they often ask if any of my former students have succeeded. Yes. Some have sold scripts and seen their work produced. Others have received paychecks and are in one stage or another of development. I take satisfaction in that.

But what gives me real pride is a student who has written a screenplay with interesting, three-dimensional characters and a strong, well-crafted storyline. His screenplay maintains a dramatic line of tension, has a nice surprise at the end of Act II, and takes me on an intriguing read through Act III until the last page where there is a satisfying ending.

*That's* an accomplishment. Selling it is the reward and having it made is the bonus No one can control what will sell, least of all the writer. I've read mediocre scripts that were bought. I've also read wonderful scripts that no important reader liked. People who have studied with me have written scripts that, were I a producer or the head of a studio, I'd grab in a second.

But there's no guarantee that someone who can get it made will like it. As a screenwriter, all you can control is what you put on the pages of your screenplay.

Don't diminish the power of that control. *Your* control! Think of it as a combination of desire, hard work and focus.

Make the process of screenwriting part of your DNA. Don't think about writing one screenplay. Think about writing ten, twenty... fifty!

Deciding to be a screenwriter is more than a choice, it's a commitment. It's a marathon.

Now go write!

D. B. Gilles

*"Life has meaning only in the struggle.
Triumph or defeat is in the hands of
the gods. So let us celebrate the struggle."*

Swahili warrior song

# Appendix
# Five Great Books
# to Add to Your
# Reference Shelf

*Adventures in the Screen Trade*
William Goldman
Published in the early '80s and still in print, this is the ultimate insider's book from the novelist and screenwriter (*All the President's Men, Marathon Man*), detailing his illustrious and often maddening career in the trenches of Hollywood.

*Bird by Bird: Some Instructions on Writing and Life*
Anne Lamott
I read this when I need a lift — when the writing isn't going well or the day-to-day business of living is getting me down. Reading this is a form of therapy for writers. Read two chapters and you'll be refreshed and ready to start again.

*The Devil's Guide to Hollywood: The Screenwriter as God!*
Joe Eszterhas
A rich resource of great insights from one of the most-produced screenwriters (*Flashdance, Jagged Edge, Basic Instinct*) of all time.

*The Writer's Journey: Mythic Structure for Writers*
Christopher Vogler
Inspired by the work of Joseph Campbell, this magnificent book is both a scholarly work and practical guide to utilizing mythic structure and archetypes in the craft of storytelling.

*Write That Play*
Kenneth Thorpe Rowe
In my opinion, the greatest book ever written on storytelling and structure. As the title indicates, the book approaches writing from the point of view of a playwright and the examples are from plays written prior to 1940. However, the wisdom and insights on dialogue, structure, and storytelling are as contemporary as if written today. Unfortunately, it is out of print, but you might be able to find it in an old bookstore or online.

# About the Author

D. B. GILLES teaches screenwriting, comedy writing, and writing for television at the Maurice Kanbar In-

photo by Allison Maggy

stitute of Film & Television at New York University's Tisch School of the Arts.

He also has taught in the Dramatic Writing Department at NYU, the Graduate Film Department at Columbia University, and the Gallatin School of Individualized Study at NYU.

He is the author of *You're Funny! Turn Your Sense of Humor Into a Lucrative New Career* and *The Portable Film School*. He is co-author of the George Bush parody *W. The First Hundred Days. A White House Journal*. He is also the author of the play *Sparkling Object*.

Gilles is also a script consultant and writing coach. Many of his students have gotten deals, sold scripts, had their work published, and had their TV scripts, sketches, and screenplays produced. He is a member of the Writers Guild of America.

■ ■ ■

Gilles is the author of the popular blog:

**Screenwriters Rehab:**
**For Screenwriters Who Can't Get Their *Acts* Together**

■ ■ ■

■ ■ ■

# To reach D. B. Gilles
# for individual script consultation,
# please visit

## Screenwritingwithdbgilles.com

### or directly via email at

**dbgillescript@gmail.com**

■ ■ ■

# THE MYTH OF MWP

In a dark time, a light bringer came along, leading the curious and the frustrated to clarity and empowerment. It took the well-guarded secrets out of the hands of the few and made them available to all. It spread a spirit of openness and creative freedom, and built a storehouse of knowledge dedicated to the betterment of the arts.

The essence of the Michael Wiese Productions (MWP) is empowering people who have the burning desire to express themselves creatively. We help them realize their dreams by putting the tools in their hands. We demystify the sometimes secretive worlds of screenwriting, directing, acting, producing, film financing, and other media crafts.

By doing so, we hope to bring forth a realization of 'conscious media' which we define as being positively charged, emphasizing hope and affirming positive values like trust, cooperation, self-empowerment, freedom, and love. Grounded in the deep roots of myth, it aims to be healing both for those who make the art and those who encounter it. It hopes to be transformative for people, opening doors to new possibilities and pulling back veils to reveal hidden worlds.

MWP has built a storehouse of knowledge unequaled in the world, for no other publisher has so many titles on the media arts. Please visit www.mwp.com where you will find many free resources and a 25% discount on our books. Sign up and become part of the wider creative community!

Onward and upward,

Michael Wiese
Publisher/Filmmaker

# MEMO FROM THE STORY DEPT.
### SECRETS OF STRUCTURE AND CHARACTER

### CHRISTOPHER VOGLER & DAVID MCKENNA

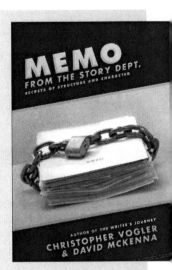

*Memo From the Story Department* is the long-awaited sequel to Christopher Vogler's immensely successful and influential handbook on mythic screenwriting, *The Writer's Journey: Mythic Structure for Storytellers and Screenwriters* (more than 250,000 copies sold). Vogler and his colleague, Columbia University film professor David McKenna, have produced an authoritative guide to advanced tools of structure and character development for screenwriters, novelists, game designers and film students. Users of the book will find a complete set of precision tools for taking their stories, step-by-step, through a quantum leap in writing quality.

"Story structure is 90% of the game in screenwriting, though it's invisible on the page. Great movies have great structure – period. Nobody understands that better, and communicates it more brilliantly, than Mr. McKenna. His insight is a key reason I'm a working writer today."
> – Mark Fergus, Oscar-nominated co-screenwriter, *Children of Men* and *Iron Man*

"The way that Vogler and McKenna tag-team this book - it keeps you on your toes. Sometimes when you're yelling in the wilderness - it's good to have two voices. Certainly they'll give you perspectives on screenwriting that you've never seen before - and in this world of multiple screenwriting book choices - that's a good thing."
> – Matthew Terry, filmmaker/screenwriter/teacher – columnist for
> *www. hollywoodlitsales.com*

Christopher Vogler is the top story analyst and consultant for major Hollywood studios and talent, advising on projects as varied as *The Lion King* and *Fight Club*. He wrote the script for the animated feature *Jester Till* and the story for a Japanese-style manga comic, *Ravenskull*. He was executive producer of the feature film *P.S. Your Cat is Dead* and has worked recently on projects for Will Smith, Helen Hunt, Roland Emmerich, and Darren Aronofsky. He travels widely to lecture about mythic structure. With Michael Hauge he produced the instructional DVD *The Hero's Two Journeys*. His book *The Writer's Journey* has been translated into ten languages and is one of the top-selling screenwriting manuals in the world.

David McKenna is a stage director, acting coach, voice-over artist and film professor at Columbia University and Barnard College. He is an expert on the films of Clint Eastwood and film genres including horror, westerns and war movies. His influential classes on screenwriting have stimulated a generation of young filmmakers and writers.

$26.95 · 280 PAGES · ORDER NUMBER 164RLS · ISBN 13: 9781932907971

# THE WRITER'S JOURNEY – 3RD EDITION
## MYTHIC STRUCTURE FOR WRITERS

### CHRISTOPHER VOGLER

## BEST SELLER

See why this book has become an international best seller and a true classic. *The Writer's Journey* explores the powerful relationship between mythology and storytelling in a clear, concise style that's made it required reading for movie executives, screenwriters, playwrights, scholars, and fans of pop culture all over the world.

Both fiction and nonfiction writers will discover a set of useful myth-inspired storytelling paradigms (i.e., "The Hero's Journey") and step-by-step guidelines to plot and character development. Based on the work of Joseph Campbell, *The Writer's Journey* is a must for all writers interested in further developing their craft.

The updated and revised third edition provides new insights and observations from Vogler's ongoing work on mythology's influence on stories, movies, and man himself.

*"This book is like having the smartest person in the story meeting come home with you and whisper what to do in your ear as you write a screenplay. Insight for insight, step for step, Chris Vogler takes us through the process of connecting theme to story and making a script come alive."*
> – Lynda Obst, Producer, *Sleepless in Seattle, How to Lose a Guy in 10 Days*;
> Author, *Hello, He Lied*

*"This is a book about the stories we write, and perhaps more importantly, the stories we live. It is the most influential work I have yet encountered on the art, nature, and the very purpose of storytelling."*
> – Bruce Joel Rubin, Screenwriter, *Stuart Little 2, Deep Impact,*
> *Ghost, Jacob's Ladder*

CHRISTOPHER VOGLER is a veteran story consultant for major Hollywood film companies and a respected teacher of filmmakers and writers around the globe. He has influenced the stories of movies from *The Lion King* to *Fight Club* to *The Thin Red Line* and most recently wrote the first installment of *Ravenskull*, a Japanese-style manga or graphic novel. He is the executive producer of the feature film *P.S. Your Cat is Dead* and writer of the animated feature *Jester Till*.

$26.95 · 448 PAGES · ORDER NUMBER 76RLS · ISBN: 9781932907360

# SAVE THE CAT!®
## THE LAST BOOK ON
## SCREENWRITING YOU'LL EVER NEED!

**BLAKE SNYDER**

## *BEST SELLER*

He's made millions of dollars selling screenplays to Hollywood
and now screenwriter Blake Snyder tells all. "Save the Cat!®" is
just one of Snyder's many ironclad rules for making your ideas
more marketable and your script more satisfying — and saleable,
including:
- The four elements of every winning logline.
- The seven immutable laws of screenplay physics.
- The 10 genres and why they're important to your movie.
- Why your Hero must serve your idea.
- Mastering the Beats.
- Mastering the Board to create the Perfect Beast.
- How to get back on track with ironclad and proven rules for script repair.

This ultimate insider's guide reveals the secrets that none dare admit, told by a show biz veteran
who's proven that you can sell your script if you can save the cat.

*"Imagine what would happen in a town where more writers approached screenwriting the way
Blake suggests? My weekend read would dramatically improve, both in sellable/producible content
and in discovering new writers who understand the craft of storytelling and can be hired on assignment for ideas we already have in house."*
>    - From the Foreword by Sheila Hanahan Taylor, Vice President, Development at Zide/Perry
>      Entertainment, whose films include *American Pie, Cats and Dogs, Final Destination*

*"One of the most comprehensive and insightful how-to's out there. Save the Cat!® is a must-read
for both the novice and the professional screenwriter."*
>    - Todd Black, Producer, *The Pursuit of Happyness, The Weather Man, S.W.A.T, Alex and
>      Emma, Antwone Fisher*

*"Want to know how to be a successful writer in Hollywood? The answers are here. Blake Snyder
has written an insider's book that's informative — and funny, too."*
>    - David Hoberman, Producer, *The Shaggy Dog* (2005), *Raising Helen, Walking Tall,
>      Bringing Down the House, Monk* (TV)

BLAKE SNYDER, besides selling million-dollar scripts to both Disney and Spielberg, was one of
Hollywood's most successful spec screenwriters. Blake's vision continues on *www.blakesnyder.com*.

**$19.95 · 216 PAGES · ORDER NUMBER 34RLS · ISBN: 9781932907001**

# YOU'RE FUNNY!
## TURN YOUR SENSE OF HUMOR
## INTO A LUCRATIVE NEW CAREER

### D.B. GILLES

*You're Funny!* is the next best thing to being in a comedy writing class. It covers the different ways to earn a living as a comedy writer, including writing sitcoms, jokes for late night talk shows, parody, stand up, and screenwriting and will help you determine if you can actually make a living writing jokes and making people laugh.

*"Fast. Funny. Informative. D.B. Gilles has written a delightful book about tapping into your inner funny. Read it. You'll laugh. You'll learn."*

> — Matt Williams, co-creator/producer, *Roseanne, Home Improvement*; director, *Where The Heart Is*

*"D.B. is a positive force for comedy. This book is a funny, entertaining, and practical guide for anyone wanting to break into the world of comedy writing."*

> — Jeff Cox, writer, *Blades of Glory*

*"You're Funny!* is one of the best books available on comedy writing with a 24 carat gold payoff-specific guidance on how to turn those skills into a profitable career."*

> — Don DeMaio, teacher, American Comedy Institute, NYC

*"You're Funny!* is the first how-to handbook that ever got me laughing out loud. A long-time student of the comedy game, D.B. knows his stuff and is damned funny in passing the secrets on. A real treat."*

> — David McKenna, co-author of *Memo From The Story Department*

D.B. GILLES has taught comedy writing and screenwriting in the Undergraduate Film & Television Department at New York University's Tisch School of the Arts for nearly 20 years. He is the author of *The Screenwriter Within: How to Turn The Movie in Your Head Into a Salable Screenplay* and *The Portable Film School*. He is co-author of the George Bush parody *W. The First Hundred Days: A White House Journal*. D.B. is also a script consultant and writing coach. He writes the popular blog *Screenwriters Rehab: For Screenwriters Who Can't Get Their Acts Together*. His new play *Sparkling Object* opened last year in New York.

$19.95 · 185 PAGES · ORDER NUMBER 160RLS · ISBN: 9781932907957

CPSIA information can be obtained at www.ICGtesting.com
Printed in the USA
BVOW02s2330270716

457065BV00040B/678/P